Fruit
of the
Vine

by Betty Dopson

Published by Lexikos

Edited by Laurie Cohn

Design and Production by Mark Adamsbaum

Cover Design and Illustration by Janet Wood

Calligraphy by Robin Hall

Set in 11 point Souvenir. Reproduced from pages generated on the Macintosh II computer and printed on the Apple LaserWriter printer.

ISBN 0-938530-44-5

Printed in the United States of America

TO CHUCK

My teacher, mentor, and friend
Who never lets me be less than the best I can be

ACKNOWLEDGMENTS

The author gratefully acknowledges the help given her by many friends in the wine community, including Louis P. Martini, Mike Grgich, Robert and Margrit Mondavi, Napa Valley Wine Library, Bancroft Library at Berkeley, Napa County Historical Society, Sonoma County Historical Society, The Wine Institute, Olivia Lasher, Arnold Santucci, Robert Boardman, Gaye LeBaron, Charles DeCrevel, Gene DeKovic, and many others too numerous to mention, but deeply appreciated.

Table of Contents

FOREWORD

When I came to Napa Valley in 1950 I knew nothing about wine. My first experience involved a Green Hungarian wine from Souverain Cellars, in Lee Stewart's time. So impressive was its freshness and vigor, its fruity zest, that it lead to more tasting. My first red was a Beaulieu Vineyards Cabernet Sauvignon, made by its master winemaker, Andre Tchelistcheff. It was regal, balanced, superb. Thus began my love affair with wine.

Since then many fine vintages have crossed my palate. All the while I was writing about wine, and reading everything I could find about its background. I found a tantalizing bit here, a glimpse there; there was no history of California wine as such.

So, stunned by my own audacity, I decided to write one. As a writer I was privileged to know the wine community in Northern California. Its people were as fascinating as their wine. Armed with this background, the assistance of many descendants of the great wine families, various libraries, museums, and historical societies, I set at the task. It was a labor of love.

Now I present to them, and to all who love wine, a story about the beginning and the ongoing of the wine industry, from its birth as a bundle of cuttings on Father Serra's mule back to the start of the Wine Boom in 1967. All that I have of skill and integrity as a writer have gone into it. I hope to have captured at least a measure of its color and drama.

The wine, the wine country, and its people continue to enchant me. They are the heroes and heroines of my story.

INTRODUCTION

By Miljemko (Mike) Grgich

My friend Betty Dopson is as much a part of the wine community as are the grapes and the wines. She has been writing about them for thirty years, with empathy and warmth. She loves the wine country and its people, and has a keen appreciation for the work and dedication that goes into making good wine. Her book has been called "history with a sense of fun." It is well researched and eminently readable.

Chapter I
Days of the Padres

*Father Junipero
Serra, who brought
the vine to
California.*

It was fiesta time at Mission San Diego—the first vintage from their new vines. This September day in 1772 Indians and Mexicans hurried about, making ready the grape press, a cowhide suspended from four corner posts set in the ground. Baskets of grapes came up, balanced on the heads of trotting Indians. As they came, a man on a short ladder carefully emptied them into the cowhide.

When it was full enough, two Indians, feet scrubbed, began the trampling. As the first juice splashed their legs, shouts and cheers went up, soldiers fired their muskets, and the brown-robed Franciscans added their cheers.

When the grapes were a pulp, the mass was put into cowhide bags for fermenting, and more baskets were emptied into the press. The vines, planted in the fall of 1769, were now bearing abundantly in this new land, thus assuring a good supply of wine and brandy. Grown and fruited from roots brought by Father Junipero Serra and his band on the long trek from the mission at Baja California, this first ripe harvest and pressing were momentous events.

It was more than three years since Father Serra, on January 9, 1769, had blessed the flags of the expedition and sung Mass to insure divine protection on the journey. The flagship *San Carlos*, loaded with supplies, had set sail earlier and would meet them in San Diego harbor.

The entourage was an impressive one—padres, Christian Indians, Mexican laborers, soldiers and officers, and the remuda of more than two hundred horses and mules. There were also cattle and oxen, equipment for house and field, roots of fruit trees, assorted seeds, and bundles of grape vines. There were vestments and chalices for the church, and a precious supply of sacramental wine in skin bags. The expedition was headed by General Gaspar de Portola; on these journeys the padres had found that the sword must always go with the cross, for there were unfriendly Indians.

Such was the coming of the vine to California. It was a long time dream of Father Serra to found a chain of missions up the coast of Alta California and to convert the heathen to the Mother Church for the greater glory of God. Father Serra was the humblest and most unselfish of men; he drove his band hard, not for his sake, but on fire for God. He pushed on to convert more heathen souls. His fondest dream was that he might be found

The spreading vines of the famed Trinity Grapevine at San Gabriel, California offer welcome shade to visitors. Planted in 1861 by Dr. David Franklin Halland, named for the Holy Trinity because of its three main trunks, this vine is one of the largest grape vines in the world.

worthy to die a martyr's death, as he recorded in his journals. He was small and slight in stature, and suffered from a sore on his leg which would not heal. At times on the march, he had to be carried on a litter, but his ardor never waned. He constantly cheered on and encouraged the Indians, whose zeal, understandably, did not always match his. Each day's journey began with Mass at dawn.

Founding a mission was a long and wearisome task. These overland treks were not the romantic journeys portrayed by fiction. Water was scarce, supposedly faithful Indians deserted, and many died. Food often ran out, and privation and pain were daily companions on the trip. Only the iron determination of Father Serra kept the group going forward during the months of travel from the parent mission in Baja California to San Diego.

Father Serra had counted on finding the San Carlos in the harbor when he arrived at San Diego, but it was many weeks before the ship arrived with its much needed provisions. Half the crew had died of scurvy and dysentery. The new mission became a hastily set up hospital camp, and a newly consecrated cemetery received many of the survivors during the next weeks.

Old San Diego Mission.

Meanwhile, the work of establishing the mission went on. New Spain (Mexico) was adept at founding missions; she had founded many in the New World. The site must be near wood and water on a rise of ground, so that arriving ships could be seen, with open fields for grazing and planting. The friars brought supplies for the year or two while new crops were being planted and grown. Among the supplies were the precious grape vines and a scanty store of wine to be carefully husbanded until a ship could bring more from Mexico. In time, their own grapes would provide the wine, without which Mass could not be celebrated.

After the vines were in the ground, they had to be tended and watered. This required Indian converts, for most of the Indians who had accompanied them had died or deserted. The padres had equipped themselves with blankets and beads to lure the Indians to the compound, which consisted of hastily erected brush enclosures to serve until there were enough hands to make adobe bricks. Here the cross was raised to mark the founding of the mission on July 16, 1769. The mission had to produce all kinds of goods without delay. Not only did it have to be self sustaining, but it had to make such things as shoes, saddles, cloth, leather, grain, olive oil, and wine to trade with passing ships in order to obtain other necessities. It was necessary to raise a plant that could produce all this from the dry, rocky soil of Alta California, and also build a church, barracks for soldiers, and housing for officers. For the Christian converts, the Mexican workers, and even for the dedicated priests, it was a Herculean task. With Father Serra already gone, advancing up the coast to found another mission, the Franciscans had to be vigilant in exercising rigid discipline over their Indian converts to get the job done.

Once the Indians had consented to join the mission community they were never allowed to leave it without permission. They were assigned work, taught the fundamentals of the Christian faith, and were required to attend church services daily as well as learn the basic skills of farming and construction.

To relieve the irksomeness of daily toil and to help encourage the Indians to reverence, every possible feast day was observed with as much pomp and ceremony as the padres could muster. There were processions, games, and celebrations. In spite of this, and of the fact that ample food was soon available, the Indians resented the loss of their freedom. In some missions the rule of the padres was especially harsh, and the Indians were virtual slaves, bound to a life of arduous toil while priests lived in such luxury as the primitive missions afforded. This resulted in many Indians escaping to rejoin their tribes. Such miscreants were hunted down and returned.

Willa Cather's book, *Death Comes for the Archbishop* describes one such incident, in the death of Father Montoya, a priest at Pueblo Acoma in New Mexico. Father Montoya was a gourmet. At a dinner given for his fellow priests, a hapless Indian servant was so unfortunate as to spill a sauce on one of the diners. Father Montoya gave the boy a furious blow on the head, which resulted in his death. The Indians of the pueblo waited until sunset, then quietly came for the priest and, carrying him to the edge of the cliff on which the church and priest's house stood, cast him to his death over the rocky side.

This retribution for injuries suffered by the Indians probably happened more than once, for in California Indians were not as docile as black slaves proved to be in the South. They were a forest people, and were never willingly made into farm laborers or construction workers.

The priests on the other hand, as representatives of the Church, felt that a life spent toiling for the faith was a small price to pay for salvation.

Meanwhile the vineyards flourished. The vines were planted to the Mission grape, probably of Mexican origin and related to the Spanish Criolla, which had been grown in Mexico for two hundred years before being brought to California. The Mission grape was easy to grow, had a sturdy vine that needed no staking, and ripened well in almost any climate in California. The exception, says Leon D. Adams in his book *The Wines of America,* was at Mission Dolores in San Francisco, where the padres imported their grapes for winemaking from missions located in sunny valleys. The missions did the industry a service in demonstrating the wide variety of favorable climates and soils for wine grapes in the state.

The wine, made by the primitive methods described, was racked into new skin bags for storage. Though everyone drank it, no one ever claimed that it was especially good. In his book *Vines in the Sun,* Idwal Jones says, "It was mediocre but useful, and the

Sutter's Fort, built in 1840-1841, where Captain John Augustus Sutter, originator of Sacramento County's wine industry, began his cultivation of native wild grapes.

Franciscans wrought their honest best with it." It served the needs of the times; life was hard, amenities were lacking, and nobody thought of wine in terms of greatness.

By 1823 the last of California's missions were centers of civilization, and also of trade and industry. They manufactured a wide variety of goods, which were traded for pots and pans, glass, lighting fixtures, musical instruments, and other things they could not make. The only wines to be had were the mission wines, and ship crews were avid customers. After months at sea, any wine was consumed with gusto.

During the period 1821 to 1833, Mission San Gabriel, presided over by Father Jose Sanchez, was a flourishing center of California industry. It made and sold vast quantities of leather, saddles, woolens, soap, wine, and brandy, all made by Indians under the watchful eyes of a well organized staff of Mexican overseers.

The Indians did not dare to be openly rebellious, but were always looking for ways to even the score with these overseers. On rare occasions they managed to get the better of them.

A young supervisor of the mission stills wrote that it was the overseer's custom to feed the stills at night, then retire to his room. When the Indians saw him go, they would uncover the still and help themselves, drinking as deeply as they pleased. This was detected, however, and padlocks were put on the covers. The offenders were put in irons. The Indians countered this with a new trick.

The wine was conveyed from fermenting vats to the storage room in barrels, with one of the heads off, the head being carried at the end of a long stick by the hindermost man. The burden was heavy, and they were permitted to set it down and rest from time to time. "Oh if this stick were only hollow," lamented one of the crew. "A hollow cane would do," answered another, "and we could take our turn carrying the barrelhead." So it was done. When they arrived at the storage room a judicious quantity of water was added before they hammered home the head.

As the trade grew, the padres were charged with misconduct. Governor Sola accused them of smuggling in liquor and other merchandise on the pretext of receiving necessary and therefore tax exempt mission supplies. This may have been true. The padres had an amazing ability to look after their own interests, as well as those of the missions. Among other misdeeds, the padres were accused of consuming inordinate quantities of wines and liquors.

All these lapses on the part of the church led to the secularization of the missions by the Mexican government in 1834. It was the theory of the mission system that, in due time, each would be self-sustaining and could flourish under the Indians without the help of mission

This drawing by Edward Vischer, made in 1865, shows part of the entrance to the Aliso Vineyards and winery, founded in 1833 by Jean Louis Vignes, California's first professional winegrower. The vineyards, covering 104 acres in what now is the heart of downtown Los Angeles, were named for the sycamore pictured here.

personnel. Although the padres pleaded that the Indians could not yet manage on their own, secularization went into effect. By the provisions of the Secularization Act of 1834, the properties of the missions were wrested from the friars and turned over to the civil government. During this transition period, much of the mission wealth melted away. Fields withered, cattle died, and unattended vineyards ceased to bear. The prudent and economical management of the church-controlled missions became wasteful under secularization.

Some of the padres, angered by the Secularization Act, actually destroyed mission property. At San Luis Obispo, San Miguel, and elsewhere, they tore out most of the vines. Vineyards and winemaking equipment were partially or completely ruined. Vines at San Luis Rey and San Juan Bautista missions were stricken by an insect pest of undetermined nature in 1838. By 1840 the Carmel Valley was deserted, overgrown with grass and brush. By 1846 hardly a vestige of vines, formerly covering scores of acres of land around the missions, was left standing.

Visiting ships were incensed that they were unable to purchase any wine or spirits in California. Actually, some of the missions did continue to produce wine and brandy for some years after secularization. But the land had been taken from the padres; it was now Mexican, French, German, and Hungarian. All were soon to become Americans, and they would dominate the wine scene for the next few decades.

The contributions of the missions to the wine industry should not be minimized. The industry owes them much. They brought the vine, proved that California was a superlative wine producing region, and they bequeathed these benefits to their successors, who would grow grapes and make wine here. They made wine of sufficient quality, even from the lowly Mission grape, and it gained a good reputation. Theirs was a profitable business, a glimpse of what the industry might one day become. They trained growers and winemakers who carried on the craft.

The untended mission buildings began to crumble. Wooden doors and windows were salvaged by the settlers, as were any other oddments they fancied. Vineyards taken over by the government were disposed of to individuals under the long list of Mexican land grants.

Chapter II
The Days of The Dons 1830-1860

El Aliso winery of Jean Louis Vignes.

Don Luis Vignes was pleased with himself on that morning in May 1837, and with good reason. He had come to El Pueblo de la Reine de Los Angeles only six years ago. At that time he was a lowly cooper eager to ply his trade in a new land which, he had heard, was covered with wine grapes. He had left his home in Bordeaux to found a cooperage business in this land of flowing wine. Good fortune had attended him.

He first found a vacant adobe, moved in, cut down the oaks which covered the land, converted them into barrel staves, and set up shop as a cooper. He had no competition; there was no cooperage in the New World. Wine was aged in stone jugs bought from merchant ships, or in clay pots made by the Indians. His success was great. He came to Los Angeles in 1831, and by 1833 he had enough money to purchase a house, 104 acres in what is now downtown Los Angeles, and to plant grapes.

These were no common grapes, but were European vinifera grapes, carefully packed and sent to California by way of Boston and then around Cape Horn. There was little or no good wine in California; made from the Mission grape by crude means it was often barely drinkable. While it was sometimes called "good" by those sufficiently thirsty, much of it was harsh, sour, and crude. Don Luis was a man blessed with vision for the future. He would change all that. With his first vintage coming on to fill the barrels in his cellar, he planned for the future—not only his own, but the great future of California wine.

He wrote to his nephews in Bordeaux, describing the new land in glowing terms. He urged them to join him, along with any of their friends and kin who could be persuaded to the venture. Vignes tended his European grapes and dreamed dreams of destiny. His pride in his venture was immense. Don Luis knew viticulture. He understood the effects of soil and climate. He watched over his vineyard with the fond eyes of a father, and the grapes flourished while he planned for their future.

Jean Louis Vignes was not the first secular winegrower and winemaker in California. Probably the first to arrive was Joseph Chapman. He was a Missourian, tall and lean, said to be an ex-pirate. His face was marked by a scar which might be a saber cut from the hazards of pirating, or more likely, by a blow from an Indian tomahawk.

He came to the Los Angeles area in 1820, the first Yankee to arrive on the scene. He worked as a jack of all trades, and thus became acquainted with Father Jose Bernardo Sanchez and with other friars at Mission San Gabriel. Convinced by their success with grapes and wine, and armed with their lore and their plants, he set out four thousand vines in 1823. However, the searing heat of Los Angeles summers, and the dry soil, discouraged this early grower, accustomed to the loamy earth of his native Missouri. He abandoned his vineyard and went back to doing odd jobs around the settlement.

The next to arrive was William Wolfskill, who came in 1836. An ex-frontiersman, trapper, and hunter from Kentucky, he had come West in 1822, traveling across country from Santa Fe, New Mexico, where he had drifted on his way to California. The band of twenty-two men included another who was to become an important figure

General Mariano Guadalupe Vallejo, founder of Sonoma and Santa Rosa, last Mexican commandant of California, and first state senator-elect from Sonoma County had revived winegrowing at Sonoma Mission in 1836. His prosperous vineyards attracted other growers to Sonoma.

in the annals of California wine—George Calvert Yount. Wolfskill was armed with a Kentucky rifle and his beaver traps, and he hunted and trapped otter. He also worked as a woodsman, cutting down timber in the mountains to the east. The lumber had to be hauled one hundred miles to the settlement, where it was needed badly in the growing community.

On his arrival in Los Angeles he had made the acquaintance of Father Sanchez, who was a fine host and offered hospitality to all comers; the Mission gardens were flourishing and food and wine plentiful. Inspired by this, Wolfskill saw an opportunity for himself in the wine industry. With money saved from his earlier enterprises he was able to purchase a vineyard. The Secularization Act of 1834 had turned the Mission property over to the Mexican government, and in time he received a generous grant of land—four square leagues, or 17,756 acres. He became a Mexican citizen to qualify for the grant, and married Magdalena, daughter of Jose Ygnacio Lugo.

Wolfskill was thrifty and prudent; he made money and persevered in the grape growing and winemaking industry. He rented out his presses, equipment, and cellars to other growers, receiving in return a percentage of the wine after fermentation. He was the first winemaker on record to ship wine to San Francisco, which he did in 1849. He remained active in the wine industry through the 1860s.

Another of the same breed was Benjamin Davis Wilson, who came on the scene in 1841, a frontiersman in a fringed leather jacket. At first he did hunting and trapping in the countryside surrounding Los Angeles. It is said that Big Bear Lake was so named for his exploit of roping twenty-two bears in the vicinity.

When he arrived in Los Angeles he planted vines and became Don Benito, one with Don Luis Vignes and other important citizens. His land was called Oak Knoll; it is now the site of the Huntington Library at San Marino. Don Benito was popular and became interested in politics; he was the first mayor of Los Angeles.

Other growers followed; Louis Bouchet, Juan Domingo, William Logan, William George Chard, and Richard Laughlin all planted grapes in the Los Angeles area. This was the center of the wine industry; in 1818 the town had 53,686 vines, and by 1831, 100,000 vines.

However, most of these early growers failed to carry on

for long. The early settlers who turned to viticulture were accustomed to a free life, surviving by their wits. Their vineyards seemed to do well, and they became skillful with the work. But grapegrowing is farming, and farming had little appeal for these frontiersmen; settling down to a life of planting and cultivating bored the more adventurous ones.

Their vineyards have left no trace. They dwindled away, or were planted over to other crops, eventually becoming building sites. Their influence on viticulture was fleeting. Winegrowing is an ancient art; California history shows that those who have done well with it have been those whose roots were deep in European soil. It remained for the French, such as Georges deLatour of Beaulieu; the German, such as the Beringer Brothers, or the Italian, such as the Mondavi family, to further the art in California. They were steeped in the classic traditions of old, winegrowing cultures, of which the backwoodsmen were as innocent as babes.

Don Luis Vignes belonged to this European group. History acclaims him as one of the most valuable men who ever came to the state, perhaps the rightful claimant to the title "Father of California wine." The date of his first vintage is uncertain, but must have been about 1837, for in 1857 he advertised wines twenty years old for sale. He was the first California vintner to age wine in any quantity. The wines included claret, muscat, sherry, and angelica.

He continued to do a thriving business. His nephew Pierre Sansevaine, also from the Bordeaux region, joined his uncle in 1838, lured to California by the glowing reports penned by Don Luis. Pierre was to find that these descriptions barely did justice to the facts. He found a vineyard of forty thousand vines, a very good cellar, and good casks. The vineyard, El Aliso, was named for a giant sycamore tree marking the entrance to Vignes' estate. The fame of its wines was soon to spread further, for in 1840 Sansevaine loaded a ship with Vignes' wines and brandies and sailed for the ports of Monterey, Santa Barbara, and San Francisco. The cargo sold for the good price of $2 a gallon for the wines, $4 for the brandies. This was the first known shipment of any quantity of California wine.

Vignes' coastwise trade was flourishing in 1842. Since it was believed that the heat of the hold and the rolling of the ship helped to age wines, they were

Senator George Hearst acquired the Madrone Vineyard at Glen Ellen about 1885. During his term of office in Washington, Senator Hearst advertised his vintages by constantly serving them at his much frequented table.

Los Guilicos Rancho, with its beautiful vineyards north of Glen Ellen, was developed by William Hood starting in 1858. By 1888 it was the largest planting in the county, yielding 140,000 gallons of wine a year.

customarily sent from Boston to California and back merely to age them. Vignes was subjecting his wines to this treatment. It is told that he presented a cask of El Aliso wine to a friend when she sailed for Hawaii aboard a ship captained by her husband. Vignes assured the lady that the vintage would be improved by the voyage, but this was never confirmed, for the gift never made port—it was so agreeable that the lady, her husband, and his officers drank it all en route.

These were the great days of the dons in California history. They stood high in the good graces of the Mexican government. Vignes belonged to his favored and distinguished group. He entertained friends, the great, and the near great, at his Rancho El Aliso. He was the biggest winegrower in California, producing some forty thousand gallons annually.

He had the pleasant habit of greeting guests with generous samples of aged wine eight or ten years old, and of fine quality. Vignes presented several barrels of his finest to Commodore Thomas Catesby Jones, saying that he would like some of it to go to President James Tyler as a gift. He wanted the president to see for himself the quality and excellence of California wine. There is no record that the gift was ever received by President Tyler, but strange things often happen at sea, things difficult to account for. Perhaps the sea voyage increased the rate of evaporation. At any rate, the gesture says much for the good public relations sensibility of Vignes.

His winemaking put Los Angeles on the map; during the decade 1840 to 1850 at least a dozen new winegrowers won prominence. California thus proved, in the first year of statehood, that it contained the richest wineland in the country.

Vignes took delight in his important role as landed proprietor and maker of fine wines. He was known as Don Luis del Aliso; his vineyard, entered by an immense gate, featured a grape arbor ten feet wide and a quarter of a mile long. It drew sightseers from far and wide. He became a civic leader in this rapidly growing town; generous to the poor and distressed, helping them with money, bread, and of course, wine.

His example, added to the Gold Rush of 1849, resulted in an unprecedented boom in grapegrowing during the 1850s. Hundreds of newcomers streamed into the state, all of them consumers of the state's products. Outstanding among these was wine. It was a status symbol on the tables of the affluent, a necessity for gracious hospitality. Miners needed it to celebrate a lucky strike; those who failed needed its consolation.

Many of the newcomers, unable to strike it rich in the mines, found grapegrowing a slower but surer way to riches. Wine sold well, and fresh grapes were at a premium in the markets of San Francisco and Stockton, near the gold fields. Improved water and rail transportation following the vast influx of population permitted still further industry expansion.

In 1855 the aging Don Luis decided to retire; he sold his El Aliso holdings to Jean Luis Sansevaine, Pierre's older brother, who had also emigrated to California under his uncle's urging. The deal involved $42,000, a fortune by the standards of that time, and the largest amount ever paid for Los Angeles real estate.

The Sansevaine brothers carried on with vigor. Almost at once they concentrated on making the first California champagne, a dream envisioned by Vignes years earlier. Pierre went to France in 1856 to study the processes, and the following year returned, bringing a skilled technician from the Champagne district. In 1857 he produced 50,000 bottles of champagne; the next year it was 150,000 bottles. The champagne was acclaimed a success, comparing favorably with the champagnes of Europe. However, much of this enthusiasm may have been wishful thinking, for it was privately rumored that the champagne fell lamentably short of its goal of excellence. California was to wait another generation for fine native champagne.

Undaunted by this costly fiasco, the brothers established wine cellars in San Francisco in 1857. In 1858 they led the state with a production of 125,000 gallons of wine, much of it labeled "Aliso." The Sansevaines owned the major part of the first large shipment of California wines to New York in 1860, and they opened the first California wine cellar there in 1861.

These activities continued for several more years. After that it appears that the brothers went through a series of vicissitudes. Jean continued at Los Angeles for a few more years, then purchased vineyard property in San Bernardino County. He died bankrupt.

Pierre fared better. Moving north, he planted wines at San Jose, where he met and married the daughter of an old Spanish family, Paula Sunol. A Northern California community is named for her family. Pierre later spent eight years in Central America, returning to France to end his days. The name Sansevaine is commemorated by a street in Los Angeles. So far as is known, with the important influence of the Vignes and Sansevaine families, winegrowing became firmly established in California.

The industry continued to flourish in Southern California for a time, but by 1860 was gradually being replaced by the northern part of the state as the prime wineland. By this time, flourishing vineyards and wineries were springing up in Monterey, Santa Clara, Sonoma, and Napa Counties, and the heart of the industry moved north.

Meanwhile, at Anaheim, twenty miles southeast of Los Angeles, the Los Angeles Vineyard Society had been formed in 1856. A group of fifty German families living in San Francisco brought land at Anaheim, dividing it into fifty twenty-acre plots. Eight to ten thousand grapevines were planted on each, and by 1858, five hundred thousand vines were growing and land was being readied for many more.

These men knew nothing about grape growing or

winemaking but were determined to establish the largest vineyard in the world. By 1860 Anaheim had assumed a leading place in grape and wine production, a place it kept until 1888, when a plant disease killed all of its vines within a single year. The ground was replanted to oranges and walnuts. The Los Angeles Vineyard Society became history.

Two other men had a great impact on the wine industry in its early years; Charles Kohler and John Frohling. Neither was essentially a grower or winemaker, although they did both. Their claim to fame came from merchandising. Kohler and Frohling knew that a product must not only be produced; it must be marketed skillfully. They believed devoutly in the future of the industry, and knew that merit alone would not sell products in any quantity—they must be merchandized. The two became wine merchants. More vineyards were being planted, more wine made. They would see that it was distributed.

Kohler and Frohling were German immigrants, musicians. They first came to San Francisco in 1853, determined to sweep the musical world off its feet. The two had some limited success, and then their musical friends became involved with them in buying a vineyard in Southern California. Soon others were working the vineyards, while Kohler operated a five hundred gallon wine cellar in San Francisco, which became known for its good, sound wines. Business flourished; the pair bought a horse and wagon to sell the products around the community. Their vineyards were expanding, and they also marketed for others. By 1869, the firm had shipped over $70,000 of wine outside the state, and established a branch office in New York. They were given the right to establish sub-agencies in all cities of the country, and they also obtained permission to set up agencies and distribution centers in China, Japan, Russia, Peru, as well as several South American cities. They purchased entire crops from large producing vineyards throughout the state. Many new vineyards were being planted in Northern California, and the Kohler-Frohling firm was the marketing agent. Kohler in particular had a flair for marketing and promoting which growers, men of the soil, often did not have. They were glad to turn this branch of the business over to experts.

The firm of Kohler and Frohling was the first major out-of-state shipper of California wine. There was by this time coast-to-coast rail transportation, and the company grew. It merged with others, and had a virtual monopoly on the wine market in the entire state. The industry expanded and flourished, due to the expertise and shrewdness of a born merchandiser, and to his firm belief in promoting California wines.

Gaza Haraszthy, eldest son of Agoston Haraszthy, copied January 1945 from a photographic copy in possession of Mrs. Harriet Haraszthy Hunt, Hollywood. Gaza, said Mrs. Hunt, never married. He was born in Hungary in 1834 and died in Nicaragua in 1878 after careers as soldier and agriculturist.

During the period of the Kohler-Frohling activities, Eastern traders vied for California wines. When they got them, they promptly put European labels on the better wines to give them more cachet in the market place. Wines of lesser merit were welcome to wear a California label, a practice which did little to upgrade the image of California wine. In fact, this image suffered from such practices until well after the Repeal of Prohibition.

Robert Louis Stevenson, in his book, *The Silverado Squatters*, quotes a San Francisco wine merchant as saying to him: "You want to know why California wines are not drunk in the States? Well, here's the answer." He opened a cupboard, fitted with many little drawers, each filled with a great variety of gorgeously tinted labels hailing from a profusion of clos and chateaux. Stevenson said, "Chateau X? I never heard of that." "I dare say not," replied the merchant. They were all castles in Spain. Not one of them really existed. False labeling is why California wine was not drunk in the States. This was standard practice.

Such was the wine industry in its infancy and pre-adolescence. It was then, as now, an industry which attracted those with an itch to do great things, who wanted to help a coming industry make strides toward the goal of excellence, and to promote the image of California wines in the world. It also attracted, then as now, the greedy and unscrupulous, bent on fast profits, with little regard for the industry's future.

History gives us the clue that the best winegrowing regions of the world are in the warm to moderate latitudes. These are also the latitudes said by scientists to be the cradle of humanity. Has civilization followed the vine, or is it the other way around?

The first man ever to taste the fermented juice of the grape must have had a shock; what had happened to his fruit juice? His delight must have made him try hard to recreate by design and purpose what had happened first by accident. He must have made a decision, then and there, to make this drink a part of his life. People are still making the same decision.

Chapter III
Vallejo and Haraszthy

The vineyard of the last Mexican commandant of California, General Mariano Vallejo (inset). The vineyard of his Lachryma Montis estate (shown as sketched after its 1851 founding) was a forerunner of the modern California grape and wine industry. Now a state museum, the buildings and gardens are well-preserved. Vallejo, who surrendered to the Bear Flag rebellion in 1846, was a close friend of Agoston Haraszthy, the father of modern California winegrowing.

General Mariano Guadaloupe Vallejo was riding high. Only twenty-six years old, he was already a very powerful man, taking orders only from the governor, Don Juan Alvarado, who chanced to be his nephew. His domain was wide, and he ruled with unchallenged power the region now divided into Marin, Sonoma, Napa, and Solano counties.

Vallejo had come to Sonoma in 1823, with his garrison of soldiers, accompanying Father Jose Altimira. As soon as the padres, soldiers, and Christian Indians got to Mission San Francisco Solano they saw to it that a vineyard was planted. The Mission buildings clustered around the Sonoma Plaza. The barracks, the Mission, and some of the other adobe structures have been restored.

General Vallejo, with an eye to the future, started his

own vineyard at once. After the secularization of the missions in 1834, General Vallejo took over the Mission vineyards to add to his own. He was energetic and forceful; things usually went pretty much as Vallejo decided. In 1834 and subsequent years he laid out the pueblo of Sonoma, then turned his attention to winegrowing. Under his dynamic direction wine began to flow from the General's press, and two years later the yield was notable for the time and place. It was, of course, the Mission grape. For another two decades this was believed to be the only foreign grape hardy enough to do well in this raw new land, and experiments with other winegrapes were still well in the future.

Vallejo built two adobe homes, one at Petaluma and one at Sonoma, besides the Swiss chalet that still remains a historical monument at Sonoma. A member of a large family, General Vallejo gave out land grants to relatives and friends, and sold them to Sonoma newcomers. He was so successful in making good wine, (even though handicapped by the Mission grape) that wine men from Europe and from elsewhere in the U.S. came to Sonoma to plant vineyards and make wine.

Among these men was a colorful figure destined to play an important part in California wine history. This was "Count" Agoston Haraszthy, a Hungarian refugee, who arrived in the area in 1856. He had fled the political scene in his native land in 1849. He tried grape growing and other pursuits in Wisconsin, but when news came of the Gold Rush in California he felt that opportunity lay West. He set out at once with his family for San Diego, where he planted vineyards and made wine. He went to San Francisco in 1852, where he planted near Mission Dolores. He eventually bought a vineyard in Sonoma County and moved his residence to that valley.

Count Haraszthy was a dashing man of many hats. He has been described as "an Argonaut in red sash, silken shirt and the velour hat of a hero in Italian opera." He was as dashing as his looks indicated. The son of an old, influential, and wealthy family, he had received an education proper to his station. He studied law, and at eighteen entered the service of the Hungarian emperor, Francis I. Following that he became an important civil servant, secretary to the Viceroy of Hungary.

He was also a country squire and winegrower. He was devoted to the cause of liberty and patriotism, and as he was never silent about his views, he was soon in trouble with the authorities. He escaped in disguise with his family, leaving behind his wealth and property, which were eventually confiscated.

The Count, who was also called "Colonel," looked every inch the nobleman and man of culture. He was dark, with fierce black eyes, eyebrows, and beard, with military bearing and proud aspect. He was fiery and outspoken, and when he threw himself into a cause, things happened. He now threw himself into grape culture and winemaking in his adopted land with the same zeal and devotion he had given his country. He became one of the most influential men ever to become part of wine history.

In San Francisco, where for a time he grew grapes and worked in the U.S. Mint, he was stacking up money for his Sonoma grape venture. In time, he bought an additional six hundred acres at a very good price. He eventually owned six thousand acres. Vallejo was a neighbor whose success in growing grapes and making wine served to stimulate the Count to even greater endeavors and enthusiasm. He had transplanted his vineyard to Sonoma, and brought in many European varieties to plant there. He was the first in Northern California to plant the European grape, *Vitis vinifera*.

These plantings began with the 160 cuttings and six rooted vines he brought with him from the South. Haraszthy demonstrated that these grapes could not only be grown successfully in California, but that they could be grown so successfully as to rival, perhaps even in time surpass, grapes grown in their native homeland. Fitting grape variety to soil type was one of his innovative ideas. He dreamed, planted, built, dug cellars, and experimented. As with Vignes in Los Angeles, he never tired of extolling the merits of his new land to anyone who would listen, and he was responsible for the immigration of large numbers of Italian, Swiss, and German colonists to this country.

During moments of relaxation he dashed about the countryside behind a coachman and handsome team, impeccably dressed, arms folded, his busy mind dreaming and scheming for the great wine empire he would create. He would stop on these trips and talk to farmers and growers, explaining his ideas. His enthusiasm for this exciting new venture knew no bounds.

Count Agoston Haraszthy.

Haraszthy built himself a Pompeiian villa on a knoll, and surrounded it with palatial gardens and fountains. His wine cellars were near by. He called his estate "Buena Vista." He throve on work. Besides growing grapes in his own vineyard and making wine, he found time to write articles and pamphlets on Sonoma's climate and suitability for grape culture. He is the author of books on grape growing and winemaking.

This indefatigable man gave such periodicals as the *California Farmer* and the *Alta California* articles urging growers to plant the new vinifera grapes. He bombarded California weekly and daily publications with series after series of articles on the necessity for better grape varieties and better vinicultural methods to produce better wine.

Haraszthy was of the French school of viniculture; slow, methodical, careful, and scientific methods in vineyard and cellar. This took into consideration *every* aspect of cultivation, *every* task of winemaking. He constructed a nursery where he planted cuttings from thousands of varieties of foreign grapes, and had the most extensive vineyards in the state.

His large cellars, tunnelled into the hillside, were made with the help of Chinese labor in less than one year. Chinese laborers would work for $8 a month whereas other workers demanded $30 or more, which made the growers of the day enthusiastic supporters of Chinese immigration.

Haraszthy put in some busy years planting new vineyards, overseeing his building and winery construction, excavating new tunnels and caves, and indoctrinating Californians to the innovative idea that grapevines do not need irrigation. He demonstrated in a practical way that superior wine was made from non-irrigated grapes.

The Count was tireless in his work of proselyting, and influenced such men as Charles Krug and Jacob Gundlach to settle near him and grow grapes in this land of sunshine.

Other innovative ideas introduced by Haraszthy included the use of redwood tanks for wine storage, and hillside planting for superior grapes. He was considered the fount of knowledge in viticultural matters. Inquiries came to him from all parts of the state, and he kept up a voluminous correspondence to all corners of the world. His three sons, Attila, Arpad, and Gaza entered the

Eleanora Haraszthy, wife of Colonel Agoston Haraszthy. Photograph received in 1947 from Thomas Haraszthy of Budapest, who claims a relationship, and said the orig. bore the notation "Charles D. Fredericks & Co., 'Speci. 587 Broadway, New York. The year when photo was t was not specified.

industry with him, and Arpad went to France to study champagne making.

To further aid the scientific establishment of sound viticulture in the valley, the Count supervised the founding of the Horticultural Society of Sonoma County in 1860, and established its experimental gardens of some sixty thousand cuttings from superior vines. But this effort died in about three years from lack of support.

Haraszthy pleaded for the establishment of a state college of agriculture, to include a school of viticulture, to give practical scientific instruction and training to all who requested it. He firmly believed that only ignorance and prejudice were responsible for California's continued viticultural backwardness.

He produced a lengthy and detailed treatise on setting out and caring for a vineyard, which was considered the best available guide to practical viticulture and viniculture. He converted many newcomers to winemaking. The Count's enthusiasm was so great that he was able to convey his own excitement about the success and future of wine in California to his readers.

To assist the budding industry, he was instrumental in convincing members of the legislature to introduce a bill in 1859 which excluded all vineyards from state tax until the vines were four years old, at which time they were in commercial bearing.

In the decade of the sixties some two million vines were set out each year in Sonoma County, due to the Count's promotional zeal and influence. He was determined that the state's new industry should be built on a firm foundation of good viticultural and vinification procedures. But inexperience on the part of growers, plus a thirst for immediate profits, made many indifferent toward choice vine varieties, good soil, climate, and viticultural methods, and thus postponed the realization of Haraszthy's dream for another two decades. This story has repeated itself many times.

In spite of the Count's efforts to disseminate knowledge about European grapes, in spite of his writings and practical demonstrations of their superiority, most growers went right on planting the old Mission variety until the 1870s. This continued popularity was the result of its continued support by the state agricultural society, never quick to adopt the new. So the Count set himself to remedy this situation. He went to Governor

John Downey and received a commission to journey to Europe and bring back cuttings of vines he believed suited for culture in Sonoma Valley.

As no money was appropriated by the state to pay for the contemplated trip, Haraszthy agreed to finance it out of his own pocket, expecting to be reimbursed by the state at the next meeting of the legislature. He sailed from San Francisco in June 1861, with the blessing of the state legislature, his own money, and a vague understanding that he was to purchase vines and fruit trees for distribution in California.

For five months he visited every major winegrowing region in France, Germany, Italy, Spain, Prussia, and England. He published a running series of articles in *Alta California,* aimed at informing grape growers and winemakers on the extent and progress of continental viticulture. These articles were later published in his treatise "Grape Culture, Wine and Winemaking."

Haraszthy happily roamed Europe, armed with letters to U.S. consuls in various countries, who put him in touch with the most distinguished vintners of Europe. He not only obtained valuable cuttings, but received detailed on-the-spot instruction in winemaking processes in these celebrated regions. This data was duly published in the California press, for Haraszthy was not interested only in his own wealth and glory, but was passionately devoted

Agoston Haraszthy home, Sonoma, California (No longer existent). Copied January 1945 from photograph of drawing in possession of Mrs. Harriet Haraszthy Hunt, Hollywood, daughter of Agoston Haraszthy's son Bela.

to upgrading the total industry in California. He was convinced it could be the greatest wine producing area of the world, and he meant to enhance and burnish the image of the industry in the state as a whole, with Sonoma County the brightest star in this glittering galaxy. He dreamed great dreams and he wanted all to share them.

He returned home convinced more than ever that the quality of grapes determines the quality of wine. He was also convinced that the same fine vines, the same care and science in winemaking used in Europe, could produce an equally generous and noble wine in California. His 200,000 cuttings and rooted vines, which embraced 1400 varieties, were shipped to California and catalogued under 499 different names. Arriving in good condition at Buena Vista, the most choice varieties were planted in his nursery. The rest were set out in vineyards. This would guarantee some 300,000 rooted vines ready to set out in the fall.

It was decided that the vines were to be distributed throughout the state on the basis of the number of representatives each county had in the legislature. This would guarantee their statewide distribution, for few counties had no grape growing. But due to bureaucratic bungling, this was never implemented, and the vines stayed in Haraszthy's vineyard.

His enthusiasm undimmed, he went ahead with his writing and campaigning for better things for the industry. *California Farmer* sponsored a program to form a cooperative for the planting of vines statewide, with an appropriation by the legislature to provide funding. It never got off the ground.

The publication also mounted a vigorous campaign toward establishing a college of agriculture, and due to these combined efforts, the University of California was founded in 1868. Haraszthy offered to teach selected men from each part of the state the several branches of grape culture and winemaking for free. Each man was to disseminate the knowledge to his own area. The properties of wine grapes, the planting, pruning, and training of vines, the racking of wines, and the organization of cellars were to be the major subjects of the new educational program.

During these years Haraszthy and Vallejo, friends and neighbors, continued to vie with each other in the field of producing excellent wine. The rivalry was always friendly;

Buena Vista Winery, near Sonoma. Main entrance to main building.

Haraszthy's sons Arpad and Attila married two of the General's plentiful daughters (Vallejo fathered fifteen children).

In 1862 Haraszthy informed Governor Downey of the expense he had undergone in collecting the vines and asked that an appropriation be passed to refund expenses already incurred to the extent of $12,000. The legislature argued and debated among its members on grounds that "it was unfair for the state to promote any one industry at the expense of the other." Then the attempt was made to get a payment of $8,457 for the actual purchase and $1,549 to Wells Fargo for transportation. This bill was shelved; Haraszthy never got a cent. He finally offered the vines for sale to anyone who would buy, and the poor distribution that resulted, plus ignorance and inexperience of the buyers, resulted in set the industry back for twenty-five years. The collection, gathered by the Count at great effort and expense and with high hopes, was sacrificed for political expediency.

In 1863 the Buena Vista Vinicultural Society was formed with the financial backing of William Ralston, a San Francisco banker who held the Buena Vista mortgages. This was a corporation hiring Chinese and other day laborers to work the vineyards and the cellar. Haraszthy's winery, with 400 acres of vineyard and 600 acres of land, became part of the Society's holdings. At this time the Buena Vista estate was the most important winery plant in Northern California, with extensive and valuable improvements, winemaking facilities unequalled in the state, and more than 150,000 European vines in bearing, which enabled the Society to begin full scale production from the start. The cellars included every convenience and requirement for making wine and brandy, among them a steam operated crusher capable of crushing 50,000 pounds of grapes a day.

Besides these assets the property had extensive quarries of red and white stone, forty thousand cords of standing timber, and five sulphur springs, all of which had good commercial possibilities. In early 1863, Buena Vista Vinicultural Society was prepared to become the major wine producer of the state. The Count put his son Arpad in charge of the cellars.

Twenty-two year old Arpad had just returned from France, where he had studied grape culture, winemaking, and champagne processes. Under his supervision, experiments with sparkling wines were begun. They were never particularly successful. The first champagne made by Arpad spoiled and had to be dumped. This is not surprising when it is known that the grape used for champagne making was no other than our old friend the Mission. Later, under the skilled hands of a French champagne maker, P. DeBanne, the Buena Vista Viticultural Society did make a good sparkling wine, "Sparkling Sonoma." It won an honorable mention at the Paris Universal Exposition in 1867.

Under the guidance of Haraszthy, who remained supervisor of the entire enterprise, the corporation rapidly increased its production and sales. Three new cellars were constructed, with nearly one hundred Chinese laboring in field, quarry, and cellar.

However, the venture was not a financial success. The talents of Haraszthy were more suited to promotion than day-by-day production. Although the annual reports continued to be glowing, scrutiny would reveal that it was becoming less and less solvent. Fluid capital was short, and an excise tax was added to wine and brandy. Demand flagged. Dividends began to be postponed. In 1865 and 1866 Haraszthy was called before the board of directors and charged with extravagance, irresponsible handling of money, and visionary experiments, a galling experience for the proud Haraszthy. Upon state investigation he was finally exonerated of these charges, but in the fall of 1866 he felt obliged to resign his post and left the corporation in understandable disgust. Although he had given so much of himself and his means to the state's viticultural enterprise, he felt, with some justification, that he had been hounded from the society he had created.

The society had many ups and downs during the next years, but never gained a position of successful operation. Corporate management tends to be more interested in quick profits than in the long slow processes of nurturing wine to its optimum maturity and excellence.

Haraszthy left Sonoma after parting from the society. Soon he was heard of in Nicaragua, where he was attempting to found a new venture—establishing a sugar cane plantation and making rum for the export trade. In 1869 he disappeared. Some thought he had simply left the scene. The most frequent story is that he tried to cross an alligator infested river and had the misfortune to fall in. At any rate, this tale seems to be more in keeping with his daring and intrepid character. A man with his dash, verve, imagination, and thirst for greatness could never die tamely in bed with his boots off.

Old winery building at Buena Vista Ranch, Sonoma, California. It was built in 1864 by Colonel Agoston Haraszthy, "father of modern California viticulture," and later extended upward. Here some of the renowned vintages of the Buena Vista Vinicultural Society were pressed and aged; wine-storage tunnels led from its rear wall into the solid rock of a hillside.

Chapter IV
Days of Napa Valley

George C. Yount.

George Calvert Yount reigned in his horse at the summit of Mount St. Helena and looked down at the valley below. The tall, rangy frontiersman had traveled over the Indian trail from Sonoma. It was spring 1831. The scene he gazed on was a huge garden dotted with wildflowers, lush grasses, and trees, and highlighted with golden mustard gleaming in the sun. It was the fairest sight Yount had ever seen. He took off his buckskin cap and said, almost as a prayer: "In such a place I should love to live and die." From that time on he was in and out of the Valley, traveling to and from Sonoma.

One morning he rode to General Vallejo's place where Indians were puddling clay, preparing to make tiles for the roof of the General's adobe. Yount said, "You ought to use shingles." "What are they?" the General asked. Yount took his axe which always hung at his saddle, and illustrating with a chunk of redwood, showed the General his dexterity by reducing it to shakes. Vallejo was impressed with the shingles, which were light and durable, and he engaged Yount on the spot to make enough for the job.

When it was done the General offered Napa Valley land in payment, which Yount was delighted to accept. "Half a league will do," he said. "Nonsense," said Vallejo, "We do not talk about half leagues here. You will take four leagues," for his domain was vast, stretching to the Sierras.

Yount was dismayed. He would need a score of Indians to work that much land, and his cash supply was nil. He had scarcely needed money up to that time; whatever he needed could be worked, traded, or bartered for. In the end they compromised on two leagues, and in 1835 Yount received his grant of land, the first in Napa Valley, from Vallejo.

"Napa" was the Indian word for plenty. To the people who lived there, it was a place of plenty, of richness and abundance, of trees, streams, and tall grasses, the bounty of nature the only resource. The Indians took fish, game, and such roots and seeds as could be harvested for food.

To the early white settlers, the Indians were on the land which they had appropriated without pang of conscience. White men scornfully called them "Diggers," because the Indians dug in the ground for edible roots, bulbs, and perhaps insects, that formed part of their diet. The hot springs at the head of the valley were sacred, having magic curative powers. They lived in harmony with nature, leaving little mark on the land even after thousands of years.

All this changed at the coming of the white man. The first, Father Jose Altimira, successor to Father Serra, had looked the valley over in 1823 as a possible mission site. He decided upon Sonoma. Father Altimira came to Sonoma from Mission San Rafael, and his zeal to make converts was so great that he had the walls of the Mission partly up before receiving official permission for the project. The Mission did own some Napa Valley land, but it was thought fit only for grazing animals.

Concurrently with these early happenings, a party of men led by William Wolfskill, the Kentucky trapper, set out from New Mexico for the Sacramento Valley to hunt beaver. Among them was George Yount. The party was forced to disband at Los Angeles for lack of funds. Members of the party continued to work their way northward. The horticultural possibilities of the northern part of the state were not overlooked by Wolfskill, who had established himself at Los Angeles, but also acquired a grant of land in Napa Valley, looking toward the future. His grant was four leagues of land on both sides of Putah Creek. Vines were planted and flourished, and wine grapes and other fruits soon became lucrative crops.

George Yount, arriving on the scene as a land grant holder, was prompt to plant grapes and other crops. That he was content to do this is rather amazing. He was a South Carolinian. Tired of home life, he had set out for the West, leaving behind his wife and three small children. Women took a chance when they married footloose, untamable men such as Yount, or the redoubtable Daniel Boone, who was no family man either. The wilderness was in their blood, civilization stifled them, and there was no keeping them anywhere for long. Yount became a notable exception, as had Wolfskill in the south.

Yount drifted north, after spending time in the Los Angeles area, where grapes were being grown and wines made, looking for something with more action. He did some fur sealing, hunted sea otter, fished, trapped, and fought Indians, letting these pursuits take him steadily northward, until he arrived at Sonoma and became friends with General Vallejo.

His title to the Napa land was contingent upon his becoming a Mexican citizen, so he was baptized as Jorge

Christian Brothers Novitiate School, winery, chapel, vineyards. Napa.

Conception Yount at Mission San Rafael. To firm up his position in the community he married a Mexican girl from General Vallejo's large family. Yount's former list of goods and chattels had stood at one horse, one rifle, and one axe. Almost overnight he was an influential Mexican citizen, proprietor of a vast acreage in the heart of Napa Valley, a well-born Mexican wife at his side.

His house, the first wooden structure in the valley, was a two-story Kentucky block house with portholes for protection against unfriendly Indians. It was surrounded by a stockade. Its chatelaine was a gracious lady. The former roughneck Yount became noted for his courtesy and hospitality to newcomers, and he assisted many of them in securing and gaining title to land.

Yount planted a vineyard and an orchard, and built a grist mill and sawmill. By 1860 he was producing five thousand gallons of wine a year. He got along well with Indians, for unusual in that day, he appears to have respected them as human beings, and they returned this with good will. They helped him as much as he helped them; they taught him to smoke-cure fish and game, and how to harvest and cure the native plants. He taught them to grow crops, shear sheep, weave, and make

This picture, at a Sonoma, California winery in the early 1870s, was captioned "Champagne Corking." It shows a shed where various processes of disgorging, perfecting the fill, and recorking were carried on. Wicker baskets shown were woven by Chinese employees of the winery; the finished Champagne was packed in them for the market. The building shown at rear of the shed is the brandy distillery operated in conjunction with the winery.

woolen clothing. Indians worked well for him, helping him with building and planting, harvesting grapes and taking them to Vallejo's winery across the mountain for processing. The market for wine was good; many of the 49ers had abandoned their dreams of gold and came down to the valleys to live and work. This provided a ready market for meat, produce, and wine, and Yount flourished.

The Land Act of 1851 threw titles of pre-act Mexican grant holders into confusion. Squatters overran Yount's ranch, took possession of his land, stole cattle and fruit, and created general havoc, while he mournfully paid the taxes. This went on until 1855, when the United States Government confirmed his title to the land.

During his later years, Yount commissioned a friend who was returning to South Carolina to look up his family. After waiting for him four years, his wife had finally married again. Two daughters, a daughter-in-law (his son had died), a son-in-law, and three grandchildren joined Yount at his home in California.

Yount gave the town its site, its cemetery where he is buried, and its name—Sebastopol. After his death it was renamed Yountville in his honor. He still remains in the valley where he had dreamed of living and dying.

There were other grape growers. One of the most influential was Dr. George B. Crane, who came for his health and bought some "chaparral" land south of St. Helena. He planted his first vineyard in 1859 with Mission grapes, and later set out another forty acres with vines imported from Count Haraszthy's vineyard at Sonoma.   These new grapes made wine which connoisseurs agreed was, indeed, promising. It was reported in the *Alta California* of April 18, 1867 that Dr. Crane had said "Twelve years ago that tract of barren chaparral land could not have been sold for ten cents an acre. By 1863, it raised in price to $125 an acre. This was for the most part unpromising soil, full of gravel and clay, yet this has proved to be the most productive for good grapes." In recognizing this fact, Dr. Crane was the first man in the valley to find that land marginal for other crops was good grape-growing land.

Dr. Crane had the second largest vineyard in the valley, the first belonging to Sam Brannan, who had one thousand acres at Calistoga. Brannan, who founded the town of Calistoga and gave it its name, was a millionaire from San Francisco and an ex-Mormon. It is reported that Sam got his start by retaining the brethren's tithes. When Brigham Young called him to account, he is said to have replied, "This money was given to the Lord; when he signs the receipt I will give it back to him." Brannan had collected choice grape cuttings in Europe, and planted them in 1857. He built a winery, a distillery, and a warehouse, and shipped his products to New York.

Other early Napa Valley vineyards included that of Frank Kellogg, three miles north of St. Helena, with a vineyard planted in 1846, which brought favorable notice from the *Alta California* in 1866. (The Kellogg mansion is still a home, owned by the William Lyman family.) William H. Nash, whose vineyard was at Calistoga, planted vines in 1852. The Thompson brothers, William and Simpson, planted six thousand vines and these were among the first known non-Mission plantings in Napa County. They had raised the vineyard to thirty-four thousand acres by 1876, but abandoned their venture soon after because the quality of grapes, and the bouquet of the wines, was inferior to that grown upon the hill lands higher up in the valley. The Thompson vineyards were in the Soscol area, where currently some very fine wine grapes are produced. The Thompsons were among the first to recognize that irrigation of grapes was unnecessary, and their contributions to the growth of the industry cannot be discounted. Discouragement, not failure, was their problem.

Joseph H. Osborn's Oak Knoll vineyard won an award in 1856 from the California Agricultural Society for the "most improved farm in the state." Today it is part of the Beringer winery holdings.

Another very successful vintner was Harry W. Crabb, whose vineyards and cellars, called To Kalon, were between Yountville and Oakville. Others were Jean A. Brun and Jean Chaix; a part of their plant is still at Oakville. The two former French cellarmasters established their vineyards and winery with great care and scientific expertise. Their vines were of the imported Haraszthy varieties and they were famed for their rare blended wines.

Another interesting old winery, now a home, is at Winery Lake, in southern Napa County. The 456 acre ranch was first planted to vines by William Winter in 1855. Its ownership passed to two Frenchmen, Michael Debret and Pierre Priet, in 1884. They built the picturesque stone winery with a medieval aspect, enhanced by a tower. It is said that having little money, they built it of stone filched by night from neighboring rock walls. Money for cement being scarce, the mix that held the rocks together was a thin mingling of sand and lime, mostly sand. They had some choice varieties of grapes, and their dream was to produce a Burgundy to match those of France. They planted, tended, grafted, but never quite achieved their ideal.

They returned often to visit their homeland. Homesick for France, they created a bit of it in Napa Valley. Feeling that nothing had such sentimental and practical value as plumbing, they imported a bathroom installation for their home. They had the faucets marked *chaud* and *froid* installed on the wrong sides, so that turn of the froid faucet would bring a stream of scalding water to charm them with Gallic inconsistency.

They owned a French poodle, and when it needed dentistry they had it fitted in France with three gold front teeth, a sight still remembered around Napa Valley.

After the French occupation, the winery was owned by German brothers who grew grain during Prohibition. Later it was a dairy barn with mushrooms grown commercially on the ground floor.

When the present owner, Rene diRosa, bought it in 1969, the building had succumbed to the ravages of time

Occidental Wine Cellar and Vineyard were owned by T.L. Grigsby, and located six miles east of Napa. He had a total of 257 acres of which 80 were planted to grapes. His production was 300 tons, and he had a 250,000 storage capacity.

and poor bonding material. DiRosa rebuilt it, strengthening the structure with steel, concrete, and timber, and planted a new varietal grape vineyard in 1961. His grapes are famous, and fine wine of the valley often bears the notation "Winery Lake Vineyard" on the label.

Another beautiful stone chateau is Chateau Chevalier winery at St. Helena. With its towers, stained glass windows, and the remains of a formal garden, it became the home and winery of the Gregory Bissonettes. It was built in 1891 by Fortuno Chevalier, a Frenchman, who was an artist in stained glass, and who is responsible for the windows. The Bissonnettes sold the winery in 1984 to Gil Nickel of Far Niente Winery, another old, restored, stone winery in Napa Valley.

It was during the 1860s that Jacob Schram came to the valley and established Schramsberg, which he operated for years, making wines of excellent quality.

The Felix Salmina family from Switzerland set out a vineyard near St. Helena in 1864. A younger member of the family, another Felix, came to the valley in 1880 and built Larkmead Winery, on Larkmead Lane. This is now the home of Hanns Kornell Champagne Cellars.

West of Oakville on a hill above the valley was the vineyard, winery, and residence of Dr. Doak. It was a beautiful complex of Victorian buildings. The mansion has been restored and is a Carmelite monastery.

Edge Hill, another mid-valley winery and residence, very complete and modern, was owned by William Scheffler, with vineyards and cellars cared for by experienced *vignerons*. He introduced the wine industry to its first automation. A complete system brought water to the home and vineyards, there was a cooperage shop for making wine barrels, as well as a brandy distillery. It comprised some one thousand acres. In recent years the Edge Hill Winery was converted to a home by Louis P. Martini.

In 1853 John Pachett planted a vineyard west of Napa, and in 1859 he erected the first stone cellar in Napa County. It measured thirty-three by fifty feet; each year he filled it with four thousand gallons of wine.

Men responsible for the growth and improved methods of viticulture and viniculture include many more. Among them was W.C. Watson, who opened the famed Inglenook Vineyard and Winery at Rutherford around 1872. Watson was producing 154,000 gallons of wine a year when he sold Inglenook to Captain Gustav Niebaum.

At Yountville, the complex of brick buildings was the former winery and distillery of Gottlieb Groezinger from Wurttenberg. He owned a huge vineyard adjacent to the winery, and made wines acclaimed for their quality until Prohibition. After Repeal, wine was made there for a few seasons in the 1940s. The buildings were abandoned until they were restored in the 1960s by a group of investors. They are now a small village in themselves, called "Vintage 1870" for the year Groezinger founded his winery.

Many growers and winemakers had implemented modern ideas which did not come into general use until much later. Among these was the conception of California wine as its own entity, not a duplication of any European wine, but a fine product that would receive world-wide acclaim on its own merits. They also stressed the idea that the finest varietals must be planted in the superior (for wine grapes) soil and climate of Napa Valley. This idea also did not come into full acceptance until studies by scientists of U.C. Davis in the 1940s and 1950s confirmed the fact that Napa Valley was the logical and rightful home of the "noble vines," and too fine and valuable to grow the lesser varieties.

The wine industry in Napa Valley flourished from its beginnings, with some slack periods, until about 1890. Then phylloxera took its toll of local vineyards, as it had in all winegrowing sections of the world. Production in Napa County fell from four million gallons in 1890 to two million in 1892.

At that time, scientific investigations which had been going on for years by the University of California researchers came up with an answer to the problem of phylloxera—grafting the European vines to the hardy rootstock of the native American grape. Whole vineyards, devastated by the plague, had to be uprooted, burned, and replanted to the grafted vines.

Combined with the depression of 1890, phylloxera devastation and an oversupply of inferior grapes dealt the industry a blow from which it took decades to recover.

What were the grape varieties grown in California during the 1860s, 1870s, 1880s, and 1890s? Among others, they included Cabernet Sauvignon, Cabernet Franc, Merlot, Verdot, Malbec, Chasselas, Hock, Burger, and Riesling.

Inglenook. Wagon in foreground, vineyards, middle, winery in the distance.

Chapter V
Days of the Great Wineries

*Cesare Mondavi, restorer
of Charles Krug Winery
after Prohibition.*

The wines of California in the last half of the 19th century now entered upon their Golden Age—their first one, since they were to know another in the next century.

Sonoma was the largest wine producing area, where the finest wines were being made under the influence of Haraszthy. With his viticultural and vinicultural knowledge and expertise, he induced those around him to adopt careful, scientific methods of selective planting, good growing practices, and painstaking winemaking procedures.

Stories of the old-time winemakers are plentiful and fascinating, for some of the great writers gave them their attention. Robert Louis Stevenson was enchanted by Napa Valley and its wines. Seventy years later Idwal Jones wrote simply and beautifully of the wine country and its personalities. For these able chroniclers the country itself was beautiful and dramatic, but the winemakers were its heart, because they worked diligently for their own time and for the great tomorrow they envisioned. Two of the outstanding among them were Louis M. Martini and Cesare Mondavi at Charles Krug. Charles Krug was a man destined to have a great permanent influence on the wine industry. A Prussian immigrant, Krug was a disciple of Haraszthy. In 1860 he sold his Sonoma County vineyard and moved to St. Helena. He had married Caroline Bale, a grandniece of Vallejo and daughter of Dr. Edward Bale. Her dowry included eight hundred acres in Napa Valley, and there Krug built his first winery in 1861. One stone wall of that winery still stands, as does the carriage house of the Krug family, now restored and an active part of the present winery.

Charles Krug was a colorful, genial man. Frona Eunice Wait describes him as one of the kindliest of men, sympathetic, generous, whole hearted. He replaced Haraszthy, in time, as the wine authority of the area. His wines and brandies were marketed in England, Germany, and Mexico until phylloxera wiped out most of his vineyard. He was an important and influential part of the industry, and served on the original Board of State Viticultural Commissioners when it was formed in 1880.

After he was ruined by phylloxera, his operations were taken over by the Moffitt banking family of San Francisco. Under their ownership the winery was run by a nephew of Krug. The operation was never successful, and nothing of note was produced. It closed during Prohibition, and after Repeal the cellars were leased to Louis Stralla, who operated a bulk winery there until 1940.

Rosa Mondavi, Matriarch of the family.

Meanwhile a Lodi grape shipper, Cesare Mondavi, began looking for a place in Napa Valley to grow grapes and make fine table wine. Cesare was convinced that the day of dry table wines was coming, and further, that this Northern California area was destined to become the home of this industry. He was a shrewd man, and all his actions were well planned and calculated. He consulted his college student sons Robert and Peter about their futures, and they both elected to become winemakers. Enology was added to their studies. Viticulture and enology were taught at the University of California, at Berkeley.

Cesare began making wine at Lodi. He bought the Sunny St. Helena winery in 1937, to give his sons a place to make the better wine he envisioned. Robert worked here while Peter continued his education. Ten years later the Krug estate came on the market. Prudent Cesare lost no time in snapping up the winery as the ideal place for their project. The deal was consummated in twenty-four hours. The Sunny St. Helena winery was sold, and the trio turned their attention to the neglected Krug estate. Bulk wine shipped in tank cars to be cellared and bottled by other wineries was the Krug winery's main business at the time of the sale. The prudent Cesare kept this business going while he prepared to rehabilitate the vineyard and restore the winery to its greatness. Only the finest of the wine produced was bottled under the Krug label, which Cesare wisely retained for the Mondavi wines. Lesser wines were bottled under secondary labels—CK, C. Mondavi, etc.

Within five years, the Krug wines were again winning medals at state fairs and exhibitions. Both Robert and Peter were working at the winery, which was enlarged

Inglenook Winery, at Rutherford, Napa Valley, at the turn of the century.

and had modern equipment installed as well as a tasting room. The emerald lawn in front of the old carriage house became the scene of important invitational wine tastings. The Mondavis also began publication of their newsletter, *Bottles and Bins*, edited by the late Francis J. Gould, a retired wine importer and connoisseur. In 1964 they inaugurated the August Moon concerts at the winery, bringing good music to the upper valley for the first time.

In 1959 Cesare Mondavi died. In Italian families it is a tradition that as long as Papa is alive, he is the boss, no matter how old, well trained, experienced, and erudite the sons may become. Cesare and Rosa Mondavi and their four children had been a warm, close family, and Rosa was the typical Italian matriarch, a devoted wife and mother, a great hostess, a sensational cook. Without formal schooling she was intelligent, well spoken, shrewd, and she also had a twinkle in her eye. She was head of the family business until her death in 1978.

In 1966 Rosa was saddened by a disagreement between her two sons which resulted in Robert leaving the family winery to found his own Napa Valley winery at Oakville. The beautiful Mission-style buildings comprise the first of an array of new wineries that began then and is still going on, although the pace has slackened. Both Krug and Robert Mondavi are makers of fine and prestigious wines. The Mondavi family added a tremendous new influence to the valley, and set the stage for new things to come as Napa Valley began to enter the limelight as home of world famous wines.

Captain Gustav Niebaum, of Inglenook, Napa Valley.

SCHRAMSBERG

Jacob Schram founded Schramsberg in 1862. He was a barber in San Francisco; after the Civil War he drove to the valley by wagon, then hiked over the terrain until he found the right spot. He bought a plot of land and planted his vineyard. While getting his vines established, he traveled the valley with razor and scissors, trimming hair and beards to make money while his wife Annie kept things going at the ranch, overseeing workers in the vineyard and the cellar.

The site is off a steep road that winds uphill through woods of madrone, fir, buckeye, and at one time, redwoods. The only redwoods that remain are in a grove out in the vineyards. It is the site of the China camp where scores of Chinese lived while they worked digging the long, cool tunnels and building the large Victorian house.

Jacob and Annie (she too was knowledgeable about wine) were noted for their hospitality, and played host to all comers. Stevenson observed that the winery was a veritable picture of prosperity, and the Schrams were fat, comfortable, and genial. Schramsberger wine was known to connoisseurs far and wide. Frona Eunice Wait, who visited them about the same time as Stevenson, says "He has the bearing of a prince, and the cordiality of a true Californian." He greeted visitors at the threshold of the mansion; they were scarcely seated before he placed before them samples of his considerable skill as a winemaker. He loved the land, his wines, and his art, and his enthusiasm for all of it was heart warming.

At the time of Robert Louis Stevenson in Napa Valley (1880), Stevenson says, "It has been a seat of the industry." He depicts the Schrams sitting cosily on their veranda, chatting with guests and plying them with precious vintages. He comments, "His serious gusto warmed my heart; to him this was a solemn office, he followed every sip and watched my face with anxiety."

Schram's son took over when he died in 1904. He made good wine there until Prohibition, then sold the place for a summer home.

There have since been two intervals of re-establishing Schramsberg as a winery, both somewhat dismal, until the coming of the present owner, Jack Davies. A Southern Californian involved with big business, he became fascinated with wine, particularly the wine of Napa Valley. He began looking for a place of his own, discovered Schramsberg was available, and bought it in 1965.

Jack and Jamie Davies and their three sons live in the Victorian mansion, restored to its former elegance. They cleaned and restored the neglected caves, and began to replant the old vineyard. Because the place had thousands of feet of tunnels, Davies set himself to become a champagne maker in the grand manner, faithful to old French tradition. Vineyards were planted to Pinot Noir and Chardonnay, and when vines came into bearing, the best professional help was sought, including Andre Tchelistcheff, French-trained winemaster at Beaulieu in its great days, and scientists from U.C. Davis.

Today Schramsberg is known for the excellence of its

Captain Niebaum's Victorian Tasting Room is in its original state.

champagnes. Davies does not plan to expand his operation, although new buildings and new vineyards have appeared. His dream is "to produce a small quantity of superlative champagne." He has already had the satisfaction of achieving his dream.

INGLENOOK

Inglenook is probably the most picturesque winery in Napa Valley, famous for its handsome chateaux. It is a many-cupolaed three-story Gothic building, of stone overgrown with ivy. Captain Gustav Niebaum, a Finnish sea captain, bought the winery in 1879, after he had acquired a fortune in fur sealing and decided to take up winemaking as a hobby. The property had a small vineyard, and Niebaum promptly replanted it and additional acreage with vines imported from the finest wine districts of Europe. Among these were Cabernet Sauvignon, Pinot Noir, Chardonnay, and Johannisberg Riesling.

At that time Captain Niebaum was forty-five years old and possessed a great gusto for life; he spared no expense to make Inglenook the model winery of California. He was celebrated for his great table wines, which he had learned to make earlier in life, and he owned a fine library on wines and winemaking. He was one of the first Napa Valley winemakers to insist on absolute, scrupulous cleanliness, and sanitation in the winery and cellars, and to advocate a more in-depth study of soils and cultivation methods. Many innovations were introduced; there was steam power to aid in winery tasks, and water was piped to every part of the winery. There were conduits to carry off waste, prevent stagnant water, and unwanted odors.

The Inglenook Vineyard, owned by Captain G. Niebaum, Rutherford, Napa County.

He tested his grapes daily as harvest approached; they were harvested at their peak, and any that were not of top quality went into separate vats to be made into brandy. The grapes entering the winery were cooled, and dust and debris blown off by a current of air, also an innovative procedure. Wines were fermented dry, and bottled aged, both of these rare at this time. He judiciously blended his wines, adopting the French method of "marrying" the different crus.

The good Captain's tasting room, at the front entrance to the winery, is a gem of 19th century art. The room is panelled and fitted in antique oak, with an elaborate carved sideboard;   soft, mellow light comes through the stained glass window, and high-backed carved chairs are around a massive center table.   Fine crystal goblets were used to serve wine to guests favored enough to be invited into the sampling room.   The Captain's tasting room is preserved intact, and is opened for viewing to the fortunate few with sufficient cachet to merit this special treatment.

Captain Niebaum could afford the luxury of insisting on quality, not quantity in his wines.   He like to say that the only wines on which he made a profit were the ones given to his friends.   His vintages received wide acclaim; they were sold only in bottle, at a time when most wines were dispensed in bulk or by the jug.

Captain Niebaum was a handsome man, used to command, and he ran his winery like a taut ship.   His employees accepted this or they left.   He was loyal and generous to his friends, courtly to ladies, and implacable to those who aroused his ire.   It is related that once, irked

The Napa Valley's famed Greystone Cellars winery is pictured under construction just north of St. Helena. The winery is a prime tourist attraction in the area. It was completed in 1889.

by a state inspector at his brandy distillery, he ordered the plant torn down the next day.

On his death, his estate went to his widow, and a nephew, John Daniel, handled winery operations. He was aided by Carl Bundschu of the Sonoma County winery family. This continued under Daniel's son, John Jr., who was in charge of the winery until 1964. In that year it was sold to Allied Grape Growers (Heublein Inc.). The new owners marred the beauty of the valley by having another building erected in front of the old valley landmark, which obscures a view of the most impressive winery in the valley.

ITALIAN SWISS COLONY

This large winery is at Asti, southeast of Cloverdale in Sonoma County. It is perhaps the most widely visited winery in the world, being just off U.S. Highway 101, on a direct route from Southern California to the Northwest. There is a big Swiss chalet-type tasting room at the front where the wines may be sampled.

The winery started as the philanthropic idea of Andrea Sharboro. An Italian immigrant who had made good himself, he saw many of his countrymen in San Francisco penniless and unable to find work. This inspired him to purchase an acreage where these men could be settled on the land.

Sharboro was an unusual man, even for his day. He came to San Francisco, a boy of twelve, in 1852. He taught children in his own night school, using books he had printed himself, when he was twenty. He made a fortune in the grocery business, opened a bank, and started several building and loan companies.

Sharboro was an altruist, a disciple of John Ruskin, with perhaps a dash of Swedenborg. He drove about the countryside until he found the right spot. The farmers were set to clearing the land, removing rocks, plowing, and planting vines. His idea was to get these families on their own land where they could grow grapes. Each worker would be given housing, food, and wine for his family. Wages of $35 a month would be paid as well, but from this sum $5 would be deducted each month to purchase stock in Italian Swiss Colony. Thus in twenty-five years the penniless immigrant would be an independent grower on his own land, a man of substance.

The colonists were uneducated men and knew little of the world of finance. They would not hear of a deduction, no matter how small, to insure their future. They preferred to take the cash and let the future take care of itself. Such improvidence made the prudent banker wince, but he accepted defeat. The colony became a private venture in grape growing and winemaking.

The winery was built in 1887, but the first wines were unsuccessful. An experienced winemaker was needed, and San Francisco druggist Pietro C. Rossi, who had a degree in chemistry, was hired to take charge. After he took over, the wines were good, and during his tenure prizes were won by Colony wines at the Paris Exposition. They were sold nationally and internationally. Italian Swiss acquired more vineyards and wineries to take care of increased productivity.

Both Sharboro and Rossi built themselves elegant homes. Sharboro's was a Roman villa, set in beautifully landscaped grounds highlighted by marble statuary. The magnificent gardens, under sycamores and palms, were irrigated by water piped from overhead. Many an elegant banquet was held on the lawns, attended by European nobility, ambassadors, and great men of both Europe and the U.S.

It was Sharboro's delight, when revelry was at its height, to have the sprinklers turned on. While his guests got drenched, he roared with laughter. History says that at least once his visitors contrived to turn the tables, and the water, on him. It does not say if he found this an occasion for hilarious mirth.

El Carmelo Chapel, a small church shaped like a wine barrel, was built nearby Italian Swiss Colony. Although there's now a larger, more conventional church next door, El Carmelo has been restored and is on view to visitors.

As time went on the two Rossi sons, Edmund and Robert, took on the family operation, and made some notable wines. Pietro was killed in an accident in 1911; shortly after the winery was taken over by the California Wine Association. During Prohibition the Rossi brothers bought the winery back and supplied grape juice and concentrate to home winemakers until Repeal. Knowing that Repeal was coming, the Rossis (in 1932) got winegrowers together in a Grape Growers League, which later became the Wine Institute, as an aid to reinstating winemaking.

The winery was sold in the 1960s to Heublin Inc., but two younger Rossi sons remained at the winery in charge of quality and production. The winery at Asti now bottles mostly brandies, and makes only the superior private stock Colony wines. The line of "pop" wine introduced by Italian Swiss Colony some years ago are made at Madera. These faintly effervescent, light fruity wines have been the means of introducing countless young people to the pleasures of wine. This winery has been sold to North Coast Grape Growers Association to expand their operation.

FOUNTAIN GROVE

This beautiful Sonoma County winery was founded by a man in search of utopia, a utopia that would work that is, for Charles Lake Harris had already founded two former utopian ventures in the East. In 1875, under the Lord's direction, he left his last location in New York's Finger Lakes district to come to California. He purchased a vineyard four miles north of Santa Rosa and made it headquarters for his Brotherhood of the New Life.

With Harris came a few of his disciples, among them John Hyde, the Missouri viticulturist; Baron Kanaye Nagasawa, a Japanese nobleman, along with another young Japanese, and Harris's housekeeper. Nagasawa was the son of a titled Japanese family whose father had him educated in England. Nagasawa was a picturesque individual; he accepted Westernization readily, but found

Far Niente (Without a Care) Winery in Napa Valley, built in 1855 and restored in 1980 by Gil Nickel, present owner.

that he preferred Scotland to England. He adopted kilts, tweeds, and had a Scottish burr in his voice by the time he became a Harris disciple; he kept up these affectations to his dying day. Tutored by Dr. Hyde and spurred on by his friendship with the plant wizard Luther Burbank, Nagasawa became winemaker at Fountain Grove.

By now Harris had a band of about sixty faithful living at Fountain Grove, housed in palatial quarters. Among them was Jane Lee Waring whom he later married. Harris traveled to England from time to time, and had a genius for making wealthy converts and for separating them from their fortunes. Lady Maria Oliphant and her son Laurence, a renowned British author, came with him to America when the Brotherhood had its utopia at Finger Lakes. It was with her jewels that Harris procured money to purchase this second of his utopias. The Oliphants followed him to Fountain Grove.

Nagasawa made some fine wine. The Brotherhood had an extensive cellar, and Harris told his converts that his wines had divine and miraculous powers. He was called "Father Faithful" by his flock, and it was his habit to place little notes besides their plates daily, adjuring them to laugh, dance, sing, and be joyous.

For a time Harris was accepted by the community. Later, however, there began to be rumors of scandalous goings-on at Fountain Grove; tales of free love among the members, and of "heavenly visitants" secretly coming at night to various rooms.

Embroiled in lawsuits and besmirched by scandals, Harris discreetly withdrew, accompanied by Mrs. Waring, and went to England in 1892. Baron Nagasawa was left in charge, and he continued to make excellent wine. Upon the death of Harris in 1906, the Baron became owner. He was noted for his fine palate and for his vinicultural wisdom.

The winery, closed during Prohibition, was preparing to re-open when Nagasawa suddenly died in 1933. His estate hired an incompetent winemaker, and the fortunes of Fountain Grove dwindled. It was sold to various owners, among them Errol MacBoyle, who hired two young winemakers from Germany, Kurt Opper and his cousin Hanns Kornell. During the 1940s these men restored Fountain Grove wines to greatness, but after MacBoyle's death in 1949 his widow let the vineyards fall into neglect. Opper quit to join the Paul Masson vineyard at Saratoga; Kornell made wine in various places until he founded his own cellars in Napa Valley. In 1951 Fountain Grove closed for good.

The handsome cut stone winery still stands, but is inaccessible to the public; it is now part of a housing tract. The only other building left, the three-story redwood cottage, was torn down in 1969. The round red barn, a Sonoma County landmark, has the word "Fountain Grove" painted on it in large white letters, and it marks the spot of the former utopia.

BERINGER BROTHERS

The two Beringer Brothers, Jacob and Frederick, appeared on the scene in the 1870s, and in 1876 built the elegant Rhine House, which was Frederick's family home. The seventeen room mansion, with its famous wood paneling and stained glass windows, was the scene of lavish entertaining and gracious living in the late 19th century.

Their close friend Sr. Tiburcio Parrott had another great estate on nearby property on Spring Mountain Road, with a winery and aging cellars behind. The Rhine House and the Tiburcio mansion were designed as replicas of the Beringer home in Rhineland, Germany.

The two families were close friends; Beringer children were named Tiburcio, and Sr. Parrott gave the Beringer winery the name "Los Hermanos." Gala fêtes were held in each other's honor, with smart carriages rolling up the curving drive to the Beringer porte cochere, or along a row of olive trees to Parrott's home, an estate called Miravalle. Both of them made wines; Parrott merely for his own family and friends, the Beringers on a commercial scale, including a claret called Margaux. The Beringer cellars still boast some of the oldest and most beautiful hand-carved oak ovals in the winery world. There is one thousand feet of stone tunnel at the winery. Pickmarks of the Chinese who built the cellars were still visible until, for reasons of safety, they were concreted over by the present owner, Nestle Company.

Beringer is still an important name around the valley. After the brothers died, the winery passed into the hands of a second and a third and finally a fourth generation of the family. It was sold to the Swiss food chain in 1970,

J. de Barth Shorb. Born in Maryland in 1842, he arrived in California in 1864. He founded and incorporated the San Gabriel Wine Company in Los Angeles County in 1882. Served as Commissioner at Large on the California Viticultural Commission from its founding in 1880 to the time of his death April 16, 1896.

making the third of the great family wineries to become the property of mega-business. The new owners keep the beautiful house and grounds in top shape, with the wines currently made by Myron Nightingale, formerly winemaster at Cresta Blanca, in Livermore Valley. He is famed as being the creator of Cresta Blanca's Premier Semillon, a famous wine of the 1950s, made by spraying the grapes, after harvesting, with spores of *Botrytis cinerea*, the "noble mold" so prized by European winemakers.

The Parrott estate is now the home of Spring Mountain Winery, an important newcomer among wineries owned by Michael Robbins, who has restored the mansion and built a new winery on the property Olive trees, more than one hundred years old, still line the drive. This is also the place where scenes from the television series "Falcon Crest" are filmed.

BEAULIEU VINEYARDS

Beaulieu Vineyards, of all Napa Valley wineries, best exemplifies the Age of Elegance that was a way of life during the early 20th century. The handsome mansion still stands, in lavish formal gardens, at the end of a long avenue of flowering plum trees. And the Beaulieu wines were elegant and greatly prized by the eminent of that day.

Georges deLatour founded Beaulieu Vineyards at Rutherford in 1883, buying a wheatfield and transforming it over several years into vineyards and a winery site. DeLatour came from Perigord in France to San Francisco as a young immigrant; he had a little money, which he promptly lost in a whirl at gold mining in Placer County.

He had studied chemistry in Paris, so he came to the Northern California wine country with a view of founding a winery for himself. It took him long years to accomplish this. He first founded the California Tartar works at Healdsburg, a firm which bought up the sediment from wine tanks to process into cream of tartar. He labored at this endeavor for sixteen years before he accumulated enough capital to begin his winery. During those years he married Fernande, a daughter of another French immigrant.

After he purchased the wheat farm, which Fernande named "Beaulieu," meaning "beautiful place," Georges traveled to France for his grapevines. He bought the finest French varieties, and built his first winery. When the grapes were ready, he traveled once more to France to secure a fine French winemaker. He brought back Professor Leon Bonnet, who directed the winery's operations for many years.

The business flourished; facilities were enlarged, and more property was bought across the road, where the winery was, and is, located. Mr. Bonnet made some excellent wines which received acclaim everywhere. When he retired in 1937, deLatour went again to France to find a winemaker of sufficient stature to keep the Beaulieu wines in the forefront of quality.

He succeeded, and brought back a Russian-born, French-educated enologist, Andre Tchelistcheff. With Tchelistcheff came much expertise, a keen knowledge of enological and viticultural methods, and great devotion to his art. On first tasting a Beaulieu Cabernet Sauvignon, Tchelistcheff predicted that this was destined to become the greatest of all California wines. He urged deLatour to give up making all other wines and devote his energies to this wine alone, for which he declared the area was ideally suited. However, it was felt that a full line of wines must be offered to national and international buyers.

During the early years of this century, the palatial home of Georges and Fernande deLatour was a mecca for the great and influential of their time. They entertained presidents, royalty, nobility, and ambassadors at their table, their elegant menage presided over by the courtly and handsome deLatour and his gracious wife. Fernande was a grande dame of the old school. The deLatours were cultured, well educated, and well-traveled, enjoying all the amenities of life.

DeLatour died in 1940, but Tchelistcheff stayed on to make wine for Beaulieu during thirty-three successful vintages. During this time Beaulieu wines were among the most sought after of California wines. Tchelistcheff also acted as consultant to other wineries, established the Napa Valley Enological Research Laboratory, and sponsored many younger men in the field—among them Robert and Peter Mondavi, and Lee Stewart. All became very successful winemakers. It is a tradition in the wine country of Northern California that those who have attained success aid newcomers in every possible way, even though the latter are sure to become stiff competition later on.

When the winery, owned by the deLatours' daughter, Marquise Helene dePins, was sold to Heublin Inc. in 1969, it saddened the entire wine world. Tchelistcheff stayed on in a consultant capacity for another year, then retired to become involved with other wineries on a consultant basis. He was honored by the American Society of Enologists, of which he is a charter member, in 1970. He was hailed as a man who had made outstanding contributions to the California wine industry, and was called "the winemaker's winemaker."

Since the new owners' takeover of Beaulieu, a handsome new visitors center has been added. Some of the old wineries, such as Buena Vista, are still active today, or have been restored. Many are gone, swept away by disease, depression, Prohibition, urban encroachment, and the ups and downs of any industry dependent on the vagaries of nature. Some have gone into corporate ownership during the years of the wine boom, which began in the middle 1960s. Only where there were strong family ties from generation to generation, plus substantial money, have the old wineries stayed in the founding families. Instances of this include the Mondavi family, the Mirassou family in Santa Clara Valley, and others.

Beringer Brothers, a pioneer California winery, was established at St. Helena in the Napa Valley in 1876. Shown here at the center are Jacob L. Beringer and Frederick Beringer, the founders. The boy is Charles T. Beringer.

Chapter VI
Wine In The Coastal Area

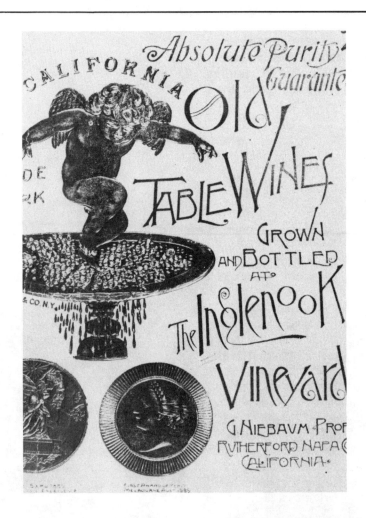

In 1777, the indefatigable Father Serra founded the Mission at Santa Clara, and the area's first vineyards were planted. Everything at Santa Clara was favorable to the vine, and the vineyards there were reported to be flourishing better than at any other mission. "They have large gardens, well supplied with every useful vegetable and even most of the European fruit trees. The fruits succeed better than at any of the northern settlements," writes botanist Archibald Menzies, speaking of Santa Clara Mission in 1792. Grapes from this vineyard were shipped to Mission Dolores at San Francisco to supplement their crops, which never produced well because of fog and cold.

According to William Heath Davis, an early trader in California wines, who published his memoirs in 1889, "the grapes yielded as fine a wine as I ever had since." Pío Pico, governor of Mexican California, conducted a retail house, producing his wines from a vineyard belonging to his brother-in-law, Jose Antonio Carrillo, of Santa Rosa Island, off the coast of Santa Barbara. When Pico retired, he placed his vineyard in the charge of Ignacio Vallejo, brother of General Mariano Vallejo.

Of early laymen who made Santa Clara County wine, the first clearly identifiable is Antonio Maria Sunol. Born in Spain, he appeared in San Jose in 1823, and within twenty years was owner of Rancho San Jose del Valle. His daughter Paula married Pierre Sansevaine, a Los Angeles grower.

Jacob Leese, a brother-in-law of General Vallejo, owned a fine San Jose vineyard. A British sea captain, William Fisher, settled on his Laguna Seca grant east of Morgan Hill, and had a one thousand vine vineyard. In 1846, Issac Branham planted a vineyard near the present-day Almaden vineyard.

Other early Santa Clara County growers and winemakers included John J. Roberts and Captain Elisha Stevens, near Cupertino, and at San Jose, Antonio Delmas from France, who imported ten thousand French shoots of choice varieties, in 1852 and 1853. These are the first non-Mission vines to be grown in Santa Clara County. This vineyard so impressed the Visiting Committee of the California Agricultural Committee when they saw it in 1856 that it was listed as "outstanding" in their report. Delmas sold many of the new varieties to his neighbors, giving the valley a start toward the development of fine wines.

In 1852, even earlier than Haraszthy at Sonoma, Etienne Thee, a winegrower from Bordeaux, planted vines along Guadalupe Creek, near the town of Los Gatos. In time Thee was succeeded by Charles Lefranc, who had married Thee's daughter. Lefranc in turn was succeeded by his own son-in-law, Paul Masson.

Paul Masson emigrated to California from the Burgundy region of France in 1879, at the age of nineteen. His ancestral family vineyards had been wiped out by phylloxera, and along with other growers, he turned to California for a fresh start in recouping the family fortunes. He attended the College of the Pacific, then located at Santa Clara. While at school he became acquainted with Charles Lefranc, and later worked for him.

A few years later Masson went to France to study champagne making. He returned when his studies were completed, bringing equipment for making champagne. He began making champagne, and in accordance with family tradition, he eventually married the boss's daughter, and the firm became Lefranc & Masson.

Later he bought the Lefranc interests and founded his own company. He won numerous awards for his champagnes, including an Honorable Mention at the 1900 Paris Exposition. Paul Masson is remembered by the wine community as an epicure and a genial host, entertaining such notables as Charlie Chaplin and the actress Anna Held, who is said to have taken her famous champagne baths at his chateau in 1917.

During Prohibition, Paul got government permission to make "medicinal champagne," and managed somehow to so enrage his competition that his plant was vandalized and his wines dumped in 1929. After this disaster, he sold out to Martin Ray, a noted winemaker and bon vivant, who continued making Paul Masson wines.

Martin Ray was a legendary character in the wine world. A former stockbroker, he became a winemaker, making wines at Paul Masson Cellars with the aid of the great winemaker Brother Oliver Goulet, from the Novitiate of Los Gatos Winery. After Ray sold Masson to Seagram in 1942, he grew grapes and made wine in the mountains west of Saratoga in Santa Clara County. It was at his estate there that Jack Davies, soon to become owner of Schramsberg, visited him in the 1950s. Davies says of the visit, "When we drove up, he was seated at the table on the veranda. He acted like Bacchus, and he looked like Bacchus, even to the vines in his hair, as he sat under a grape arbor covering the veranda."

The party sat down to lunch, served with Martin Ray wines, and, as Davies remembers, they sat there for hours, lunch merging into dinner with no appreciable line of demarcation. So impressed was Davies that he bought a vineyard in partnership with Ray. However, he found that being in partnership with Bacchus did not work as well as dining with him. Davies soon sold his interest in the vineyard and bought Schramsberg.

Meanwhile Ray continued making his wines, which he claimed were the only great wines in America, and selling them for astronomical prices.

When Seagram bought Paul Masson in 1942, it was

a time when California wineries were being snapped up by hard liquor interests who wanted to share in the huge wine profits they saw coming. When the wine explosion of the 1960s erupted, Seagram began marketing Paul Masson wines, and made it available worldwide.

Paul Masson Cellars was the first winery to bring music to the famous "vineyard in the sky" in the mountains above Saratoga. The contour of the land forms a natural hillside amphitheater in front of the Old Mountain Winery. This is a beautiful and picturesque building which had some of its components brought from Spain via Cape Horn in the old sailing vessel days.

Since 1958 weekend concerts have been held here each summer, where noted artists perform for the delight of music lovers as well as television audiences. These concerts are sold out months ahead, and the proceeds benefit college music scholarships. Other than these performances, the Mountain Winery, a state historic landmark, is off limits to the public.

Paul Masson Cellars can claim another distinction—it may boast of being the state's oldest winemaker, since its owners have produced wine continuously since Thee's first vintage in 1855.

Beaulieu—Chardonnay grapes (hand of Maynard Monahan)

ALMADEN

Hedged in by housing tracts, Almaden Winery is located on Blossom Hill Road in San Jose. It's a huge sprawling winery which exhibits a founding date of 1852. Of this once-great vineyard, only thirty acres remain. They contain the handsome Lefranc-Masson villa and formal French gardens and the small original adobe and brick cellar in which Almaden wines were first bottled. Almaden champagnes are made there now. It is a pleasant and picturesque sight. The real winemaking operation goes on in a large bustling cellar adjacent to the original holdings.

The first wine named Almaden was introduced by Henry Lefranc about 1900. The winery closed during Prohibition and opened after Repeal.

Almaden was founded very early in winemaking history by Theophole Vache, who established a commercial vineyard near Mission San Juan Bautista in 1848. Known as Cienega Winery, it later became the property of William Palmtag, mayor of nearby Hollister, who produced wines that won medals at European expositions in the early 1900s. Dr. Harold Ohrwall of San Francisco was a later owner, and in 1908 he shared ownership with Professor Frederic Bioletti of the enological school of the University of California. During Prohibition the winery itself was closed, but it sold fresh grapes to home winemakers. There were two thousand acres of vines and eight bonded wineries at Repeal.

It opened after Repeal under Charles Jones & Associates. In 1941 Louis Benoist, a wealthy San Francisco businessman, bought the property as a spot to entertain his friends. These fun-filled, roistering days are graphically described by Mary Lester, then his public relations head, in her entertaining book *Hand Me That Corkscrew, Bacchus.*

Benoist enlisted the services of wine importer and wine writer Frank Schoonmaker, who became his wine advisor. He has been advising Almaden owners ever since. Benoist planted more vineyards, but after World War II the firm began to lose money. Urban developers began to buy bits of land from the vineyards, and today all but a small tract of land is in housing under the name of Almaden Estates.

The Benoists sold their winery in 1967 to National

Distillers. The new owners have planted additional vineyards in Monterey County. Now Almaden makes more money than under the Benoist regime, but things under corporate ownership are not the same, mourns Mary Lester, who left Almaden after the sale. It's not nearly so much fun, she says, as when the jolly Benoists held forth there, pressing their champagne on all comers.

MIRASSOU

Another Santa Clara Valley winery that began concurrently with the development in Sonoma and Napa Counties was Mirassou. This San Jose winery has been the property of one family for five generations. In 1858 Pierre Pellier brought vine cuttings from France, each carefully protected by insertion in a cut potato to keep it moist on its journey. Three years later, after the cuttings had been started in his brother's nursery, he planted his vineyards and built a cellar.

Pellier's son-in-law, Pierre Mirassou, succeeded him, followed by Mirassou's son Peter. Peter's sons Edmund and Norbert are now owners of the winery, and their four sons and a son-in-law are operating the family business.

Until 1942 all Mirassou wines were sold in bulk. They had some labels printed and sold bottled wines on a very limited scale, entering some in State Fair competitions. They received gold and silver medals, and connoisseurs began talking about, and buying, the wines. In 1966 a line of premium bottled wines under the Mirassou label was introduced to the trade. During recent years, Mirassou vineyards have expanded into large acreage in Monterey County. All their wines are now vintage dated and labeled as to the vineyard of origin, and are much admired by wine buffs. The Mirassou family and their wines command tremendous respect in the state's wine community.

CRESTA BLANCA

Livermore Valley in Alameda County was the scene of early winegrowing and winemaking. Charles Wetmore founded his famous Cresta Blanca cellars there in 1880. Wetmore was a journalist, and had gone to France in 1879 to report on the Paris Exposition for the California Viticultural Society. He wrote some startling articles

This photograph of Pierre and Henrietta Mirassou was taken in San Jose shortly after their marriage in 1881. The couple was the son-in-law and daughter of Pierre Pellier, founder of the family winegrowing tradition which today is being carried on by his great grandsons, Edmund and Norbert Mirassou, at their Evergreen winery.

James Concannon, founder of the Concannon Vineyards in Livermore. Born 1847, died 1911.

following this trip, stating that most French wine imported to the United States was adulterated *vin ordinaire,* and denouncing San Francisco restaurateurs for featuring these European wines while selling the finest California wine under counterfeit French labels.

Wetmore became the executive officer of the State Board of Viticultural Commissioners, and then decided to get into the act himself. He bought 480 acres of Livermore Valley land, set out his vineyard and named it Cresta Blanca for a nearby cliff with a white crest. His cellars, according to the custom of the time, were dug into the mountain, to maintain a cool temperature.

Using his French connections, Wetmore went to France and obtained from one of the owners of Chateau d'Yquem a selection of rare cuttings used to make the famous Chateau's blend—Semillon, Sauvignon Blanc, and Muscadelle Bordelais.

In Wetmore's vineyards, these vines produced vintages that won Cresta Blanca two gold medals in the Paris exposition of 1889.

Half of the cuttings Wetmore imported were planted in the vineyard of a friend, Louis Mel, the French owner of El Mocho Vineyard. Mel later sold El Mocho to Karl Wente, giving that winery some of the fine vineyard stock Wetmore had brought from France.

Cresta Blanca made a number of wines that were famous before Prohibition. After Repeal they were again at the top of the list, under the ownership of Wetmore's brother Clarence, and later under his chief salesman, Lucien E. Johnson. The latter sold Cresta Blanca to Schenley during 1941, and soon the singing commercial of Cresta Blanca began to be heard on the nation's radios.

Cresta Blanca made wine history in 1956 when winemaker Myron Nightingale and enologists from the University of California devised a method of inducing *botrytis* in Semillon and a Sauvignon Blanc grapes by spraying them with the spores of *Botrytis cinere,* which grown naturally on grapes in the Sauternes area of Bordeaux, as well as in some places in California. The luscious, hand-crafted wine which resulted was called Premier Semillon, and was hailed as "breaking the French monopoly on one of the gourmet treasures of the world."

Even this breakthrough could not keep Cresta Blanca afloat, however, and in 1965 it closed. In 1971 Schenley sold the Cresta Blanca label to the Guild Wine Company of Lodi. Nightingale left to become chief winemaker at Beringer Brothers cellars in Napa Valley, which had just been acquired by Nestle of Switzerland.

Now a new winery in Mendocino County is selling wines under the Cresta Blanca label. The winery, called Cresta Blanca, is owned by Guild Winery and Distilling Company.

WENTE VINEYARDS

The Wente Winery at Livermore is large, and its wines are distributed nationally. A new winery and tasting room have been built recently. The winery was founded by Karl Wente from Hanover, Germany, who began his operations in 1883, when he acquired an interest in the fifty acre vineyard. He soon expanded his plantings to three hundred acres. The soil in the vineyards is thin and gravelly, and seems ideally suited to the production of superior white wines, although they currently produce some notable reds as well. Karl learned winemaking from Charles Krug in Napa Valley. His two sons Ernest and Herman took over the vineyards and winemaking operations at Wente's after graduating from University of California School of Enology and Viticulture. Herman was famous for his ability as a winemaker.

Historical photograph of the Warm Springs Vineyard and Winery in Alameda County, owned by Josiah Stanford, brother of Senator Leland Stanford, prior to 1900.

After his death in 1961, Ernest's son Carl became head of the firm. Needing room to expand, three hundred acres were planted in Monterey County.

Prior to Prohibition, all Wente wines were sold in bulk. During the dry era they made altar wines for Georges deLatour of Beaulieu Vineyards, and sold much of their crop as fresh grapes. After Repeal they began bottling wines, producing some that put them in the front of the world wine scene. They enjoy considerable prestige today as makers of fine wines, and even their jug wines are considered worth a trip to the winery, the only place they are available.

CONCANNON

Near Wente Vineyards, on the same road, is Concannon Vineyards. The founder of the winery was James Concannon, who came from Ireland in 1865 at eighteen, working his way west while educating himself at night school. Arriving in San Francisco, he first worked as a salesman for rubber stamps, up and down the Pacific Coast. As a devout Catholic, he learned from Archbishop Joseph Alemany that there was a profit to be made in the making of altar wines for the church. In 1886 Concannon bought a farm and planted imported French vines, which was the customary thing by that time. Concannon's vineyards flourished. Phylloxera was lying waste the vineyards of Napa and Sonoma Counties; growers of Livermore Valley jealously guarded their vines and complained bitterly when the experimental vineyards at Berkeley were established by Dr. Hilgard to work on his methods of phylloxera eradication. Fortunately the winds that might have carried the aphid across the mountains to the undamaged vineyards of Livermore Valley were kind, and the pest never arrived there.

Concannon planted the French wine grapes and sent many thousand cuttings to Mexico, where formerly the Mission grape had been the only one grown for wine.

Altar wines were Concannon's main products, and he was fortunately able to go on producing them throughout Prohibition. By this time the winery was in the hands of Joseph, the founder's son.

Today the winery, (in the the hands of James and Joseph Concannon Jr.) still devotes a large part of its production to altar wines, sold mostly to Catholic clergy. Concannon wines are largely white varieties, but his best is said to have been his St. Julien, a suave Claret. However, in 1936 the use of the name "St. Julien" was prohibited (except for wines from Bordeaux) by a new federal labeling regulation. Captain Joseph was annoyed by this regulation, and withdrew his great wine from production.

As in the Wente vineyards, the soil at Concannon is ideally suited to the growing of superior white wine grapes, and many of them are made. However, some of their finest vintages are red wines of the claret type.

E & J GALLO

This winery, the largest in the world, is at Modesto in the San Joaquin Valley.

Ernest and Julio Gallo worked as boys in the Gallo family vineyards near Modesto while attending school at Modesto Junior College. They wanted to found a winery. The year was 1933 and Repeal was focusing new attention on the wine industry. The public library had a wealth of winemaking pamphlets by the University of California scientists. The two boys bought some redwood tanks and a grape crusher, and, using Gallo vineyard grapes, made their first wine. It was successful, and Ernest went to New York and sold the entire vintage in bulk. Two years later they built their first small winery on a creek bank outside Modesto.

For years the Gallos made only bulk wine, but they planned ahead to a future when they would make good bottled wines and sell them under the Gallo label.

Today, with huge facilities at the same location, the brothers are making a large part of all the wine consumed in the U.S. The largest of the winery's vast array of huge steel tanks holds one million gallons.

There are bottling works, a bottle and cap factory, and research laboratories. In the Gallo laboratories many of today's noted enologists served an apprenticeship; they are said to surpass in equipment and sophistication those of U.C. Davis. Vast warehouses hold Gallo jugs and cases of bottled wine. None of this is open to the public.

The aim of Gallo was to supply the nation with good mass-produced wine under a reliable label, and they have succeeded. The San Joaquin Valley wines did not, at first, come up to this standard. The Gallos began to eliminate their defects by introducing and adding to them wines brought from Napa and Sonoma Valleys, where a growers' cooperative made wine from grapes grown in a large number of small vineyards. This system, together with plantings of the better grape varieties from the University of California at Davis, has made Gallo wines very acceptable, low priced wines.

Their Hearty Burgundy has won national acclaim as a very good and palatable wine at a very moderate price. It is made by blending free run juice with a judicious amount of press wine to step up the acid content and give it character.

They have introduced some innovative new wines, such as Thunderbird and Ripple, and they make a Charmat process champagne and a brandy. They have ventured into other fields in making fruit wines such as Boon Farm Apple Wine.

Gallo is a family owned corporation, and family members are directors of the firm. Ernest does the marketing, Julio has the vineyards and wineries in his charge. Both brothers taste their wines daily, and all decisions affecting the firm are made jointly.

Josiah Stanford, brother of Leland, planted 350 acres of vines and constructed a winery on land purchased by his brother in 1869. In 1889 Senator Stanford deeded the Warm Springs vineyard to Josiah Stanford.

Chapter VII
Wine Carries on in Sonoma County

Norman Tower, Korbel.

Korbel Champagne Cellars at Guerneville is both old and famous for fine champagne. The three Korbel brothers bought it in 1862, a wooded tract of land covered with a stand of virgin redwood, immense trees whose stumps are still visible here and there in the vineyard. The Korbels were cigar makers, and these majestic giants were ignominiously logged off and made into cigar boxes.

After the trees were gone, twenty years later, the brothers sought other uses for the land and planted vines, intending to make champagne. They started their project in 1886, in a cellar made of bricks baked in a homemade kiln. Their champagne was made with the assistance of French winemakers, and they turned out some notable sparkling wines from secretly blended cuvees.

The Korbel mansion stands on a hill above the winery, and is currently used as a guest house. Behind the winery is an old brick tower, a landmark said to be a replica of a Bohemian jail where one of the Korbels had suffered an unjust incarceration.

The three Heck brothers, Adolf, Paul, and Ben, purchased the cellars in 1954. They are the third generation of a winemaking family. They make champagne by the slow, time-honored French method, taking seven years from vintage to cork pop. During the tenure of the Hecks, the champagne has retained its fine reputation and cachet.

Adolf Heck has the distinction of having invented a mechanical riddling method, which has been patented. Instead of turning the bottles by hand every day, it is now done automatically by the flip of a switch.

A story is told of three Korbel sisters, old ladies who were the last of their family. Early in the Heck regime, they came once a month in their chauffeur-driven limousine to get their supply of champagne. Each time they would bring back empty bottles, neatly packed in the original carton. One of the Hecks protested, "You know, you don't have to bring them back." The little ladies consulted with each other and then the eldest said, "But mayn't we bring them back if we want to?" "Certainly," said the surprised Mr. Heck, "but would you mind telling me why?" "Well," said the little lady hesitantly, "we just don't want the garbage man to know how much champagne we drink."

Jacob Gundlach, one of the founders of the Rhine Farm (1856) in Sonoma County, Ca.

Buena Vista Winery. Statue in cask room (immediately inside main entrance. Room lights out due to temporary power failure).

A few years ago Adolf Heck and his son Gary became sole owners of the cellars.

The German winemakers, Jacob Gundlach and Walter Bundschu, bought land near the city of Sonoma around 1860 and set out some four hundred acres of good vines. Their Rhine Farm became noted for its good viticultural practices and healthy vines, and their Bacchus wines were celebrated for their quality. But phylloxera was no respecter of greatness, and the vineyard fell prey to the pest in the 1880s. However, the owners went ahead boldly, at immense expense, to tear up the old vines and replant their acres with high quality vines grafted on the resistant native rootstocks which, by that time, had been found to be the only remedy for eradicating the pest.

They went ahead making good wine for twenty years, until the earthquake of 1906, which delivered the coup de grace to the venture. They had extensive warehouses in San Francisco, filled with wine, and these were totally destroyed, as well as the Sonoma County winery and cellars. The partners abandoned the project, and the winery lapsed into inactivity until 1973, Then a great grandson of Gundlach, Towle Bundschu, rebuilt the winery, incorporating into it the one remaining old stone wall. He replanted the vineyard, and is producing excellent wines. The wines are prime varietals and they are distributed under the old Gundlach-Bundschu label, although no Gundlachs are presently connected with the winery.

Joshua Chauvet, at Glen Ellen, was one of the most influential winemakers and growers in Sonoma's early history. He came to the area in 1856, buying up land until he owned a large portion of the town of Glen Ellen. He established his vineyard and winery in 1877, some twenty years later. He piped water from his numerous springs to the town, and built a grist mill, a water-operated crusher and press, and installed a steam-operated system of winery equipment. His old water wheel, a Sonoma Valley landmark, has been restored, along with several of the old buildings, at Jack London Village.

Chauvet was very successful with his wines and brandies. Madame Chauvet was as enterprising and determined as her husband. She was an intrepid lady, and fond of a drink. When her husband had to go away on business, he deemed it prudent to lock the winery and distillery, and the one barrel of brandy left outside was hoisted high up in a tree.

The story goes that, giving her husband a farewell embrace, she waited until he was out of sight. Then she repaired to the house and took a rifle from its case in the living room. Pioneer women were notably good shots; they had to be able to defend themselves from frontier dangers. Madame Chauvet was no exception; taking careful aim as Joshua had taught her, she put a shot neatly through the brandy barrel, and filling buckets and pitchers, was able to drink her fill.

Just north of the town of Glen Ellen was the winery and vineyard of Captain J.H. Drummond, known locally as "the Laird." His 125 acres of grapes produced wines that won thirty awards at fairs and expositions. Drummond had imported his own special vines from Chateau LaFitte and Margaux in France. His claret was particularly famous; "sumptuous," said the connoisseurs. Half of each vintage went to the Bohemian Club in San Francisco, the other half to customers in Europe. In 1888, Frona Eunice Wait describes DunFillan as "an exquisetly clean stone cellar." These great vineyards have sadly fallen before the developer's bulldozer.

Another intrepid lady was Mrs. Kate Warfield, at Ten Oaks in the Agua Caliente area. The winery was established by Kate and her husband, Dr. J.B. Warfield, and after his death, Kate carried on alone, the only lady vintner of her era. With energy and determination she upgraded the vineyard, grafting French varieties of grapes on the old Mission stock and won prizes for her wines at expositions and fairs. She had the most modern of winery equipment, and such extra frills as oak barrels with nickel-plated hoops and the ends painted lavender with gold lettering. In addition to her talents in the field of winemaking she was an outstanding home-maker, doing fancy needlework and making her own fashionable gowns. While her wines were winning awards in Europe, her jams and layercakes were winning blue ribbons at the State Fair. She was hospitable, and enlivened local society with her charm and wit.

The Warfield vineyard was planted in 1859, two hundred acres in extent, and replanted about twenty years later to such varieties as California Chateau Lafitte, Clos Vougeot, Chateau Yquem, Sainte Macaire, Gros Maucin, Tasmat, Hermitage Riesling, and Burgundy. The grapes

Luther Burbank, plant wizard, and Baron Nagasaki, winemaker at Fountain Grove Winery.

and their wines were named for the area from which they had come, and varietal labeling did not come until many years later.   Most of these wines were blended.   It is recorded by Frona Eunice Wait, in the 1889 printing of her book *Wines and Vines of California*, that Kate won a first award for her Riesling at the California State Fair.

Quando un bicchiere di vino invita il secondo.....il vino è buono.

S. Sebastiani 1902

Sebastiani—Carved barrel in fermenting room.

Schramsberg—Dusty wine bottles in cave.

Samuele Sebastiani was another winemaker who worked and saved for years to make his dream of founding his own winery come true. He arrived in California from Tuscany in 1898 and got a job making cobblestones for San Francisco streets. With a staunch faith in his dream, he finally accumulated enough money to buy the old Milani winery in 1904. His winery, in downtown Sonoma, has been remodeled, enlarged, and equipped with modern machinery for crushing and winemaking by his son, August, who succeeded him as owner of the winery after his death in 1944.

August was a great admired of his father, and he carried on in Samuele's footsteps from 1944 until his death in 1980. Both of August's sons, another Samuel and Donald, began working in the family business as soon as they graduated from school. The chauvinism in this notable wine family is in the best Italian tradition. Grandfather Samuele is everybody's ideal. He was a much loved man, as well as a leading citizen of the town, where half the buildings are named after him.

August became another important man in his turn. He was known for several things, one of them being his collection of birds. He had a home aviary, where he had some ninety species of doves—his specialty. He also had a bird sanctuary for ducks, geese, and swans, and many other birds were given liebensraum by this ardent bird fan. Grain for birds was high on the list of August's priorities.

He was an early riser, driving out and feeding and enjoying his birds in the morning. He also like to have a cup of coffee with his cronies at a corner cafe before going to the office. His trademark was his pinstripe overalls; he was rarely seen in any other garb. He believed in his country, his work, and his wines, and he had a grassroots charisma which everybody felt.

Chapter VIII
Old Timers in Napa Valley

This is Ho Po (sometimes spelled Hoe Poe), a San Francisco labor contractor who furnished Chinese workmen to the Buena Vista Winery in Sonoma. Under the direction of Agoston Haraszthy, the Chinese bored through solid rock to create Buena Vista's famed wine storage tunnels.

In the period from about 1860 to 1910 many wineries got their start. Some are still in operation; some have given way to housing developments and other land uses. Those still in operation have weathered many changes, drought, depression, disease, and the earthquake of 1906 which wrought disaster as far away from San Francisco as the wine country of Sonoma and Napa counties.

Many of these wineries were started by immigrants from Italy, Switzerland, Rhineland Germany, and France. A perfect example of an old-time Italian family winery is Nichelini Winery, in Pope Valley founded by Anton Nichelini, grandfather of the present owner, in 1890. He came from a rural section of Switzerland near the Italian border and homesteaded a tract of land in Napa County.

Anton built a stone winery, using stone from the surrounding hills, with lime and sand for bonding; it is still strong and sound. Having land and a winery, Anton needed a wife to help him, and arranged for a mail-order bride to be sent from Italy. Family legend states that when it was time for the young lady to leave for California she fell ill, so her sister went instead. Anton accepted the substitution with equanimity; what he needed he got in Angelina. She could cook and sew, work in the house and vineyard, was strong and willing, and could bear sons and daughters to carry on after them.

In this casual way Anton took a wife who labored beside him for years. He built a redwood house on top of the hillside winery, where they reared twelve children. They planted the vineyard, and when the grapes ripened he made his first wines, in the old-time way he had learned from his father.

Early customers were men working at the many magnesite mines in Pope and Chiles Valley, where two hundred Italian immigrants toiled for wages of $1 to $1.25 per day, plus board and wine. The standard ration of wine was from a half to a full gallon of wine per man per day. No man had to go dry while the Nichelini winery was operating.

Angelina helped out in many ways. She baked loaves of crusty bread in an outdoor stone oven and sold them to hungry miners to eat as they drank their wine, happy for a touch of home.

When wineries closed during Prohibition, Anton ignored such nonsense and continued to make and sell wine. Why should he not make a living in the family tradition, growing grapes, making and selling his wines to his thirsty neighbors? A family story is that "Mama got busted for selling a gallon of wine for 35¢, and since she had a houseful of children, Anton went to jail in her place." Eventually he was apprehended, arrested, fined, and forced to close. After Repeal, he returned to making wine, but was unable to obtain a license because of his criminal record. His son came into the picture as the licensee, but the son was not interested in the family business, so his grandson Jim Nichelini, the present owner, became his grandfather's partner. A fourth generation is now active in the winery. The wines are shared with visitors, and poured on the deck behind the cellar, for there is no room inside—it is taken up by tanks, barrels, and winery gear.

Another winery of the period was Chateau Montelena at Calistoga. It was built in 1882 by Alfred A. Tubbs, founder of Tubbs Cordage, ship outfitters in the days of sailing vessels. He traveled to Europe to bring back cut stone, marble, and carved wood for his mansion and winery, as well a plans by a French architect.

At the foot of Mount St. Helena, the location is picturesque and beautiful. The winery is built into a hillside for coolness, and some of the walls are over three feet thick. The building has turrets and battlements with arched Gothic windows. Tubb's French winemaker, Jerome Bardot, made some fine wines until Prohibition brought wine operations to a close.

The Tubbs property was sold to a Chinese family in 1959, the Yort Franks, and was used as an elegant residence. Frank landscaped the grounds in the Chinese manner, with a lagoon, moon gates, islands topped with red lacquer pavilions, and a curving red bridge. Swans, ducks, and geese swim gracefully on the willow-fringed lake. This spot is now the scene of elegant winetasting and other gatherings.

In 1966 the property was sold to a group of investors who reopened the winery, which had been closed since Prohibition. Their desire was to make wines of international note, and they secured the services of winemaker Mike Grgich. Grgich was trained at the University of Zagreb School in Enology in Yugoslavia, and had served an apprenticeship in some of Napa Valley's most prestigious wineries. Chateau Montelena was now furnished with the finest and most modern of

Mayacamas—Lower entrance, main winery building.

Inglenook—Cellars.

winemaking equipment for Grgich, who brought a high level of quality to Chateau Montelena wines.   One of these, a Chardonnay 1973, won an award in Paris in 1976.

Another California wine, a 1973 Cabernet Sauvignon from Stag's Leap Cellars, also won an award the same year.   This had world-wide implications;   it was the first time that California wines, judged by Frenchmen in competition with French vintages, had received such acclaim, and the world became aware of what Californians had known for some time;   California wines were getting better and better all the time, and France might well look to her laurels.

After several successful vintages, Grgich left Chateau Montelena to construct his own winery at Rutherford in 1977.   Bo Barrett is the present winemaker at Chateau Montelena, and one of the winery's owners.

Freemark Abbey, just north of St. Helena, is an ivy-covered cut stone building dating from 1895, and for the information of history buffs, it was never a monastery.   The name was composed by former owners using parts of their own names to construct a title.   It was built by two Italian immigrants, Charles Forni and Alfred Poggi.   The sandstone came from a quarry near Glass Mountain off Silverado Trail, and was cut and shaped by use of hand axes.

It was built for Alfred Forni, a cousin of Charles, who operated it as Lombarda Winery until Prohibition.   Then it went inactive for a time, eventually passing into the hands of the Ahern family, who first bottled wine under the Freemark label.   Presumably the venture was not too successful, for the winery again lapsed into inactivity.   It passed through various ownerships and at one time was used for the making of preserves and jams.

In 1966 it became the property of the present owners, a group of Napa Valley growers headed by the young old-timer Charles Carpy.   Carpy's Bordeaux-born grandfather, another Charles Carpy, owned the Uncle Sam Wine Cellars in Napa at the turn of the century, when it was one of 142 wineries in the county.

Under the guiding hand of the famed wine consultant Bradford Webb, Freemark was given the best stainless steel tanks and the most modern equipment, and the firm began turning out some fine wines, greatly prized by connoisseurs.   Their pedigreed grapes are from the valley's finest vineyards, and Freemark shows what can be done by dedicated winemakers who have the finest grapes and the best equipment for their endeavors. Freemark continues to be one of the most highly respected names in Napa Valley.

The winery building is handsome and elegant. The front part is a restaurant, behind it a candle factory. New buildings have been added for the winery operations.

The Louis Martini Winery, just south of St. Helena, is the creation of one of the area's most colorful and dramatic winemakers. Coming to San Francisco from Genoa at the age of thirteen, Louis Martini began his career working for his father, who sold fish. As Louis grew up, his father, who had always been a backyard winemaker, sent him to Italy to study winemaking at a fine school of enology and viticulture in Alba. When he returned he began making wine, working for other wineries to gain experience, and soon started his own backyard winery at Hunter's Point. In 1907 he succeeded in making a good wine, which he sold from his fish cart along with clams and mussels.

Louis later moved to Fresno and bought the Acampo Winery. He was making wine there when Prohibition came, but he had the faith of all good Italians that such an unnatural law would not last long. During those years he made medicinal and sacramental wine, waiting out the inexplicable madness. In 1925 he bought a Napa Valley vineyard and built a utilitarian winery near St. Helena. For eight years he quietly and unobtrusively made and aged his best wines there. At Repeal, he alone had good aged wine to sell.

In 1940 Louis moved his family to St. Helena. He bought more land and planted vineyards over a large area, to get the grape flavors from various soils and microclimates, all of which have their special character. He loved to walk over his vineyards, for he had an eye for the esthetic.

In Angelo Pellegrini's book, *Americans by Choice,* Louis is pictured as he was in his prime, dining robustly, drinking wine with gusto, enjoying family, friends, home, work, with an earthy yet urbane zest and love of life. He is shown working in the winery, exchanging with co-workers the "flashes of temper that, among Italians, is a sign of love, virility and health." He is quoted as saying then, as he did all his life, that to make great wines we need men of devotion, skill, and time—that is all. All else we have.

Louis Martini was a giant of a man, blond and blue-eyed, with the volatile temperament of his breed. At eighty-five he was still strong and at his office every day, for he was still "boss." Although he turned over the running of the winery to his son Louis, another big blond, in 1960, his word was still law in the winery and the vineyard. His memory and foresight were as prodigious as his capacity for enjoyment and love of life. He died in 1980.

Time was kind to Louis Martini. When a very old man, he said he would not have the temerity to give advice to the young winemaker. He said that if a man wanted to make good wine, he should study, work, learn, be immune to the ups and downs of fortune and public taste, and be happy with today's achievement while striving toward a greater tomorrow.

There is now a large, modern visitors' center, and tasting is no longer offered in the old winery among the tanks and barrels. This is missed. There is always a certain charm about drinking wine in the cellar where it was conceived, gestated, and born.

A very different kind of winery is Mayacamas in the hills above Napa Valley. It might be considered inaccessible by a timid driver, for the road to it climbs tortuously up the slopes of Mt. Veeder some twenty-six hundred feet. Forty acres of terraced vineyard cling to its steep slopes. Veeder is an extinct volcano, and in its crater stands a three-story stone winery built in 1889 by John Henry Fischer, a pickle merchant from Stuttgart. He built the winery and planted the vineyards, calling it Mt. Veeder Vineyards. His attempts at growing grape varieties such as Zinfandel and Sweetwater are described by Idwal Jones in his book *The Vineyard*. This is a story worth reading for its realistic depiction of a place and a time whose character has changed little from that time to the present.

Fischer sold the property at the turn of the century. It was allowed to run down and fall apart during Prohibition and was not reclaimed until 1941 when it was purchased by Jack and Mary Taylor. The distillery became a comfortable home, and the winery was renamed Mayacamas, a name common in the area, for it is the name of the mountain range that parallels the valley. It is also the name of an Indian tribe that occupied the valley in the days before the white man. It is said to mean "howl of the mountain lion."

During the next twenty years the Taylors planted the vineyards to Chardonnay and Cabernet Sauvignon at great expense and with endless toil. This couple gave the winery a legacy of fine wines through their extraordinary foresight and devotion, and have left a mark on the land and many palates.

In 1961 the Taylors, who had myriad other business interests, began commuting between Napa and New York, and offered stock in the winery to customers at $10 a share. This enabled the winery to double its small capacity. However, absentee ownership took its toll of quality in the long run. The winery was purchased in 1968 by Robert Travers, a Stanford graduate with U.C. Davis training in enology.

Travers had also had an apprenticeship at Heitz Cellars under master winemaker Joe Heitz. In the interest of achieving excellence he has limited his production to three wines, hoping by doing so to improve those wines. He has done well. His Late Harvest Zinfandel has received wide acclaim, made as it was by accident in one of his early years at the winery. He was unable to be there, and it is a tradition in wine country that picking cannot be started unless the master is there.

Travers continues to plant, wrestle with rocky hillside soil, and lose one grape stake in three to its resistance. The shy bearer vines are always quality wine grapes, and produce an even smaller yield on the rocky slopes, but the quality makes great wines. Mayacamas is one of the most beautiful wineries to visit, with its woodsy environment which is the home of deer, bobcat, and the occasional cougar. Buzzards soar below as the visitor sits on the deck overlooking the valley. The mountain has the quiet charm of all wild places, and is worth the climb to get there.

Greystone at St. Helena is an old Napa Valley landmark, and it has been the home of Christian Brothers Winery for some forty years. The building was built by William Bourn about 1900, to house and age the valley wines for growers and winemakers who were feeling the pinch of hard times and needed to sell their wine. Bourn paid them for the wine and it was kept and cellared until it could be sold more advantageously. Greystone has had many owners since then, one of whom bought it in 1931 for $10,000.

The Christian Brothers own the winery and vineyards at Mount LaSalle, built in 1903. This is also the site of

Kornell—Carved door to cellar.

their Novitiate school, where young men are trained for the work of the Order. This lovely spot, on a mountainside west of Napa, is worth the climb it involves. A new building replaces the old winery, which burned several years ago. At this location, with its winery, school, and chapel surrounded by vineyards, the Angelus bell rings out and the brothers, between Matins and Vespers, make many varieties of dependably good wine.

Greystone was used as the Brother's aging cellars, with two-and-a-half millions gallons of aging wines stored in its immense interior. It was also a very popular visitors center. However, as of 1984 the building was found to be unsafe in case of earthquake, and it was reluctantly closed. It is now reopened.

Brother Timothy, cellarmaster at Christian Brothers, is almost as much a valley landmark as Greystone. He has been head winemaker at the winery for more that thirty-five years, and is probably the most photogenic, most photographed wine figure in California. He is noted as a fine winemaker, with a discriminating palate which is invaluable for blending. The wines are blended for consistency, and are always very good and very drinkable, without great difference from vintage to vintage. During the past few years, some of the best of the Christian Brothers wines, such as Pinot St. George, have been vintage dated.

Another old Napa Valley winery was Larkmead, originally owned by Lillie Hitchcock Coit, of Coit Tower fame. After Lillie returned to San Francisco the house burned, and the winery and vineyards were sold to François Saviez from southern France. In 1894 it was sold to Felix Salmina from Switzerland. This was at a time of depression in the industry, when phylloxera had taken its toil and many growers were not replanting their vineyards. But Felix had faith in the future and bought more acreage. He planted it to vineyard and made good wine at Larkmead. The winery building was of wood when Felix became the owner. In 1906 he hired stonemasons to quarry sandstone in the nearby hills, make blocks, and construct the present winery. The building is foursquare, one hundred feet by one hundred feet, two stories high, with a cupola on top.

Grapes were crushed at Larkmead by hand-turned rollers, an innovation introduced by Felix Salmina. White wine was bottled and sold, and red wine was sold in bulk or by the jug. This went on until Prohibition. After this

California section in the Viticultural Department of the Horticultural Building at the World's Columbian Exposition, Chicago, 1893.

hiatus, during which Felix ran a hotel in St. Helena, Larkmead began production again.

Larkmead under Felix made fine wine, among them a memorable one made from the Petit Sirah grape. Aided by his nephew Frank Salmina, Felix operated the winery and tended wines and vines in a way that earned Larkmead wines a place of respect in valley annals.

On Felix's death in 1940, Larkmead went from owner to owner until it was purchased by Hanns Kornell, whose name appears earlier as making wine at Fountain Grove. In the story of California wine, names appear and reappear, like golden threads in a colorful tapestry, as men who dreamed of making great wine moved about in their quest for the right time, place, and circumstances.

Hanns Kornell is becoming a legend in his own time. He came from Germany, a member of a winegrowing and winemaking family. He had worked as a youngster in his grandparents' vineyard, cleaning bottles in the cellar. He had learned the art of tasting. After high school he went to the University of Geisenheim Enologic Institute. He worked in wineries in France, Germany, and England.

With the threat of war coming in 1939, he came to America. He hitchhiked from New York to California, where he worked for a time at Fountain Grove in Sonoma County. From there he went on to make champagne in Missouri. Returning to California in 1952, he leased an old cellar in Sonoma and opened his first champagne cellars. Selling by day, bottling and riddling by night, he amassed funds to buy Larkmead, and founded his own cellars in St. Helena in 1958.

Hanns Kornell himself would not deny that he is a man of destiny. He has always believed in himself, and in his ability to found and maintain a champagne dynasty. He has never been afraid of hard work, nor afraid to dare greatly. All this has made his cellars a very successful venture. He has made some excellent champagnes. In 1958 he married the daughter of a long-established winegrowing family, Marilouise Rossini. The two Kornell children, Paula and Peter Hans, are enthusiastically involved with the family business.

Champagne is made in the *methode champenoise* at Hanns Kornell, fermented in the original bottle, and maintains a very high standard of quality. He also makes champagne for several other wineries. He believes profoundly in the future of Napa Valley, and in his own place in that future. He has a tremendous vitality and love of life that transmits itself to everybody around him.

Chapter IX
Phylloxera and its Aftermath

Professor Eugene W. Hilgard, Dean of the College of Agriculture, University of California 1890. Professor Hilgard was a pioneer in experimental and scientific research for California viticulture.

In spite of their romantic image, grape growers are farmers. Farmers deal constantly with the realities of weather and what it can do to crops. Next to weather, insect pests have the greatest effect on crop success or failure.

In 1855 the insect phylloxera attacked vineyards in France. It was an American native, brought to Europe, scientists believe, from California vines imported for grafting, and spread, slowly at first, then rapidly to almost every winegrowing country of the world, leaving havoc in its train.

Sonoma County vines were first in California to feel the ravages of this pest. Although the insect had been slowly killing vines for some time, it was 1873 before it was identified. It threatened the entire industry before it was brought under control in the last decade of the century.

Phylloxera, an insect of the aphid family, has over thirty varieties, including the deadly *P. Vastatrix. Vitis vinifera* (the European grape) is highly susceptible to its ravages. Its presence is first seen as stunting growth, reducing leafage and lowering fruit production. Galls appear on the underside of leaves; small rootlets show knotty swellings. These finally rot and turn black. Meanwhile, the insect is busily extracting sap just as the rose aphid attacks the family rose garden. The vine finally dies as a result.

This insect has an involved life-style, well-suited to its survival and spread. A single egg is laid on the bark of a vine in fall by a fertilized, winged female. The egg passes the winter there, hatching in spring into a wingless female. This insect creeps into an opening leaf bud, forming a gall on the young leaf. Eggs are handily produced parthogenetically (without male sex participation). From these eggs, other wingless females emerge; later in the season another winged form appears, which lays eggs that hatch into both male and female insects. Sexual reproduction and fall migration result, and the cycle starts over again.

All this is done by nature to assist the aphid to survive; what the grower must do to survive is up to him. At the time he was baffled as to how to combat the ravages of the insect, because it appeared in such large numbers almost before the Northern California infestation was known to exist.

Phylloxera ravaged the vineyards unchecked, killing so many vines that growers gave up in large numbers, turning to other crops that were not vulnerable. But the phylloxera disaster was not all bad. Some good resulted, besides finding the remedy, which took about twenty years of experimentation by scientists at the University of California. At that time, their experimental vineyard was located on the Berkeley campus.

The insect was eventually controlled by the same means as it had been in France earlier—by grafting the European vines onto phylloxera-resistant rootstock. The most effective of these rootstocks proved to be the Midwestern wild grape root.   Those which saved the California vineyards came chiefly from Missouri, oddly enough by way of France, for the French had already fought their own battle with the pest.   They had been using the rootstock in the replanting of their vineyards for several decades, and had a more plentiful supply on hand than did its native state.

Two men are credited with stopping the havoc and finding a remedy for infestation.   The remedy consisted of pulling out infested vineyards and burning them, then replanting to vines grafted on the rootstock of *vitis rupestis*, the Midwestern wild grape.   The two men are Professor George Husmann, a professor of horticulture at the University of Missouri, and Professor Eugene Hilgard, later dean of agriculture at the University of California.

Husmann had made a visit to California in 1881, and was taken with the idea that California was the future home of the wine industry.   Soon after that he emigrated to California to live, grow grapes, and become a winemaker at Napa, which he did, happily, until Prohibition closed his winery.   He wrote several books, among them *The Native Grape and the Manufacture of American Wine,* a dreary enough title which belies the somewhat poetic flights it contains, such as "I firmly believe this continent is destined to be the greatest wine producing country in the world.   America will be, from the Atlantic to the Pacific, one smiling and happy Wineland."

His co-worker, Professor Eugene Hilgard, headed the University's research.   He had experimented with grape growing in Mississippi and Michigan before coming to California in 1875.   The phylloxera problem was his first challenge.   In addition to his work in the control of phylloxera, Professor Hilgard made other contributions to wine improvement.   He called for (but didn't get) large, modern wineries, methods, and equipment, slow fermentation at controlled temperatures, and the bringing of science to all phases of vinification.

He soon recognized two of the other critical problems of the time; the adaptation of grape varieties to different climates of the state, and the fact that California as a winegrowing area was warmer than the winegrowing areas of Europe, and needed to be treated differently.   The warmer weather in California had resulted in high sugar grapes with low acid, which would not ferment completely dry.   They made sweet, flat wines, which spoiled easily.

Hilgard attacked the varietal problem in a masterly study of composition and quality of grapes and the wines of the major varieties of grapes, growing in different locations. His studies established the importance of grape variety to quality of wine, and it had a salutary effect on the generally high quality of grape varieties in the state's vineyards before Prohibition. Hilgard was quality-oriented, which did not endear him to some of the more commercially minded wineries.

The State Board of Viticultural Commissioners took on the task of trying to change the public attitude about California wine. They sponsored conventions, published translations of important European enological treatises, carried on educational activities, and wrote reports on industry statistics and problems. Although the board was short-lived, its work was important, and is carried on at present by the Wine Institute. Legislation for which this board was responsible attempted to halt the spread of phylloxera by quarantine, and the present state plant quarantine regulations, with which most Californians have had a brush at some time or other, date from this early attempt at pest control.

Hilgard promoted other ideas that were new to California wine-growing as well. One was, if grapes stay on the vine too long, they acquire too much sugar in relation to acid, disturbing the delicate balance responsible for great wine. California vintners, with their European backgrounds, had been accustomed to thinking that grapes must have all the sugar they could get, because in the German and French sun-starved wine countries it was usually necessary to do everything possible to increase sugar content in wine grapes before harvest. In some vineyards in Germany, it is still customary practice to carry stones and rocks up in baskets to place around each vine, so that the sun, warming the rocks. could be released to the vine over a few more hours each day. Hilgard discovered that in California too much sugar was the problem. He was one of the first to realize the part that right sugar-acid balance plays in determining wine quality.

Winehaven, once the world's largest winery, was closed with the advent of Prohibition. Located five miles from Richmond, California, the Winery was located at this site after the California Wine Association was burned out in the San Francisco fire of 1906.

Like other scientific winegrowers before him, Hilgard favored thinning heavy crops, so that the vine might not have more berries than it could ripen.

In examining the effects of phylloxera on the industry at the time it was taking its toll of vineyards in Northern

California (1880-1885), it is possible to see some positive effects.

For one, it came at a time when overplanting had been the order of the day, with depressed prices as a result. The same was true in Europe. The shortage of imported wine, plus the shortage of California wine to replace it, resulted in a price rise that was beneficial to winemakers who had been able to stay in business.

The dread of disease and its threat to the entire industry influenced the state legislature to establish a State Board of Viticultural Commissioners once more, and a department for viticultural research and instruction at the University of California. Although these two bodies constantly fought with each other during their short co-existence (the Commission was abolished in 1894), it did lead to the control of phylloxera.

Section of California's viticulture exhibit, the Golden Wine Temple, at the Louisiana Purchase Exposition, St. Louis, 1904.

Most Northern California grapevines are grafted on phylloxera resistant roots today. The two in use are St. George, a *Vitis rupestus* variety from the Midwest, and AXR, a hybrid resulting from a cross between Aramon, a *vinifera* grape, and St. George. In some few places, notably in Lake County and Monterey County, ungrafted vines are being grown on their own vinifera roots, a calculated risk that some growers are willing to take if the land has never before been used for grape growing, as is the case in most of these areas.

There were some fine wines made before the phylloxera destruction in the state. Among them were wines from Inglenook, Miravalle, Fountain Grove, Senator George Hearst's winery at his Madrone Vineyard in Sonoma County, the Warm Springs vineyard of Josiah Stanford, brother of Leland, near San Jose, and many others. Some of these are mentioned in Frona Eunice Wait's book, *Wines and Vines of California*, published in 1889. She was a reporter on the *San Francisco Examiner* and a noted wine buff. Her descriptions of some of these famous wineries, palatial mansions, and well-kept, well-managed wine estates give present day wine fans a look at the Victorian splendor of another and more elegant day.

Following the phylloxera outbreak, and the consequent replanting of vineyards on resistant rootstocks, the entire industry was upgraded by planting to better varieties of grapes. In terms of Northern California, this now means the varieties that grow superlatively well here cannot be grown so well anywhere else in the state, perhaps in the world, including their native lands.

These include, but are by no means limited to, Pinot Noir, Chardonnay, Cabernet Sauvignon, and Sauvignon Blanc. There is also Zinfandel, which grows fantastically well in Northern California vineyards, and makes some very interesting vintages. Zinfandel has come into its own in the past decades as a top varietal wine. Earlier Zinfandels were mediocre wines, for the most part, and nobody expected a Zinfandel to be great. With more carefully selected strains of vines, and with more imaginative winemaking procedures, the vintner now seeks to bring out the wine's latent great qualities. It now takes its rightful place beside Cabernet Sauvignon and Pinot Noir as one of California's most distinguished red wines.

Better grapes are needed to make better wine, for the winemaker cannot, by any amount of dedication and skill, compensate for lack of quality in the grapes. Poor wine can be, and sometimes is, made from good grapes; it is utterly impossible, say the great vintners, to make good wine from inferior grapes.

The fact that better grapes and better methods made better wine was demonstrated in 1900, when American wines won three dozen medals at the Paris Exposition. Finally California wines were recognized for themselves, not hidden under a foreign label. Their quality put them in competition with the finest wines of the world, and they were even judged by French winemakers.

Better grapes were the end result of the phylloxera infestation. There were also better informed winemakers, and better equipment in wineries, during the post-phylloxera period, which lasted from 1900, when the pest was finally controlled, up to 1920, when an even greater plague struck—Prohibition.

Some growers, their vineyards gone and destroyed by the disease, did not replant. But most of them did. Those who did were mainly descendants of winegrowing families, with roots reaching back to their European ancestry, and unable to view any other way of making a living. Hence it was the more dedicated, less dollar-oriented growers who survived and carried on, planting fewer but better grape varieties.

Another scientific discovery of the late nineteenth century was made by Louis Pasteur in regard to spoilage of wine. He found it was due to aerobic micro-organisms producing acetic acid, turning wine into vinegar, and that it could be prevented by keeping wine out of contact with oxygen. At the same time, the industrial revolution brought new methods, and new machinery was devised for crushing grapes. These made it possible to handle the wine without undue exposure to air.

Pure yeast cultures to secure clean fermentation were introduced, and fining agents to produce greater clarity and stability came into use.

In 1890 the California Wine Association, financed by San Francisco businessmen, constructed a large modern aging and bottling plant at Richmond, California. They bought wine from all over the state, often making their own prices and sold them under their own label. Although it was said that they never sold a bad bottle of wine nor a great one, they did establish some innovations that upgraded the quality of wine. The Association had one of the first chemical laboratories for testing and analyzing wine. It was not until some years later, after World War II, that the chemical laboratory, large or small, simple or sophisticated, became an accepted part of every winery.

As grape vines began once again to cover the Northern California landscape, the government was induced to offer incentives to those who would replant, giving them free land, tax advantages, money for research, and other benefits.

In this pre-Prohibition period, the University of California began to play a larger role in grape growing and winemaking. The University's enological and viticultural departments had by this time been moved to Davis.

In 1846 the town was named for Jerome Davis, a member of the intrepid Bear Flag party. Davis settled in Yolo County in 1852, and the town was named Davisville after him. It was later shortened to Davis. In 1906, when the industry was recovering nicely from the trauma of phylloxera, the University of California bought the Davis ranch and opened a practical farming school there. The school opened with forty students. Since then enrollment has climbed to more than twenty thousand students in more than forty-five departments. It covers six square miles, is the largest University of California campus, and has its own airfield for scientists to fly to experimental stations and other campuses where agricultural subjects

Mayacamas—View of hillside vineyards.

are taught. As time went on, the School of Viticulture and Enology assumed greater and greater importance, and became a training ground for the numbers of vine men who desired to learn more about their craft, and to have their sons educated in the scientific aspects of winemaking and growing.

Professor Hilgard continued as head of this department for years. In 1889, he hired a young man, Frederic Bioletti, as his cellar foreman. Bioletti, an Englishman with an Italian name, later succeeded Hilgard in charge of the work on wine.

Some great names are among his students, such as William Cruess, the world's foremost food scientist and Albert Winkler, who attained equal fame in the field of agriculture. Bioletti's coming marked the beginning of greatness for the University's School of Viniculture and Enology, and its fame and prestige has became so great, worldwide, that sons of French winemaking families are now often sent to Davis for a part of their learning, for it has earned a place among the world's great schools of enology. The School of Enology at Fresno State University has also won acclaim as a great school for winemakers.

In the story of wine in California it has always seemed to be that, no matter now dismal the picture might become, no matter how much the individual grower or winemaker might suffer in personal disaster, there was something in the vine that was always tending upward, toward greatness. Setback after setback, price drop after price drop, the tenacious grape has never yielded. Sometimes in eclipse, sometimes burgeoning, it has gone to greatness.

On the eve of Prohibition, the wine industry was in upswing. Prices were good, new vines were growing better grapes, better trained winemakers were producing better wines by using more efficient equipment and methods. Things were trending upward, with no end in sight. The future looked bright.

Chapter X
Dark Days for the Vine

Rhine House (1883), Beringer Winery, St. Helena—Exterior.

Prohibition in the United States, and its aftermath, made many strange bedfellows. It affected the entire country, but nowhere was it more disastrous than in California, where wine grape growing and winemaking was a leading industry. It is difficult for people today to understand just how it could happen; however there have always been those who, not desiring to drink themselves, are determined that nobody else should do so either.

Perhaps we may admit that at least their motives were worthy. Some were led by genuine altruism, believing sincerely that alcohol was the cause of all the troubles of mankind since Pandora's box. We had yet to shed our own Puritan inhibitions, and the belief that if something is fun, it must be at least a little bit wrong.

No doubt it irked the abstemious one, sipping a chaste and innocuous glass, to see others imbibing, enjoying wine and the feeling of community that drinking wine gives to a group of people. There is something about sharing wine with friends, or with people who enjoy wine, that makes for conviviality and a free exchange of ideas. It has nothing to do with being intoxicated.

People rarely become intoxicated on wine; its image is that of being the beverage of the civilized drinker. Except for winos and derelicts, nobody drinks wine to become drunk, for as the late Ogden Nash pointed out, "Liquor is quicker."

Our Puritan heritage came out strongly in those who came to be called "drys," and it made them determined to do away, once and for all, with something that contributed to the degradation of mankind, and to save people from themselves.

For one hundred years before Prohibition, do-good characters were passing among the population, aiming particularly at the young, trying to lure them from all alcoholic beverages. Sunday school children were a fruitful field; they signed up in droves to forego Demon Rum. Another good source were old soaks, who were often approached in saloons, bleary of eye and tangled of tongue, by dainty but stern ladies who harangued them on the perils of their drinking habit. The men usually ended up sobbing in remorse. This usually lasted about ten minutes, or until the next round of drinks.

Everybody has heard of the redoubtable Carrie Nation, with the glittering eye and sharpened axe, who made her way into saloons hacking at bars, breaking glass, and wrecking whatever was in her path. She was usually accompanied by a group of earnest and dedicated women, determined to save their erring brothers from their own folly.

Carrie was not alone. The Women's Christian Temperance Union, formed in 1875, held town meetings, marched, and broke up friendly drinking in taverns. They were the Women's Libbers of their day.

Marching in protest is not entirely new. The Anti-Saloon League, which numbered many prominent Americans among its ranks, was also active, but more sedate, and used lectures and pamphlets to distribute information.

In spite of the efforts of these groups, and of many other determined drys, National Prohibition came on with a shocking suddenness, setting the whole nation back on its heels, especially California, where people consumed the greater part of the wine made in the state.

The people of California, particularly those with an European background, were accustomed to a culture where wine was a way of life and babies were given a slightly diluted glass as soon as they were weaned. It was difficult, if not impossible, for such people to see any sense at all in prohibiting the making and selling of wine, any more than if it were bread, or any staple of life. To such people, bread and wine were affinities; chunks of fresh, crusty bread torn from a loaf and accompanied by draughts of good wine, were an everyday occurrence, a mini-celebration to mark all kinds of occasions. To such people Prohibition seemed hysterical nonsense.

There have always been those who wanted "temperance," which they took to mean total abstinence, not moderation, inflicted by law on state and country. By the time National Prohibition took effect in January 1920, thirty-three states were already dry. Kansas had been dry for years, as had Iowa, Georgia, Oklahoma, and other Southeastern states. This is the area jeeringly referred to by liberal thinkers as "the Bible belt," inferring that wine as a beverage is condemned by the Scriptures, which it is not.

Many wine lovers believed then, and believe now, that wine drinking tends toward temperance, meaning moderation. Dr. Salvatore Lucia, Professor Emeritus at the University of California, at San Francisco Hospital, as well as other medical men, see merit in the use of wine in treatment of patients who need its beneficent effects. Dr. Lucia especially recommends it as "a balm for autumn," implying that it helps older people to relax and forget their aches and pain.

One of the most insidious parts of the campaign of the drys was the way they kept references about grapes and wine, and the industry in general, from the history books. So completely was the wine industry shut out of recorded history that the history books today, even those written as recently as this decade, make little mention of California's most lucrative and important industry, the industry which also gives the state its greatest stature and prestige.

The brainwashing that went on during this time included the attempt to remove from all literature, even the classics, any reference to wine. They did succeed in having medicinal wines dropped from the United States Pharmacopeia. The Department of Agriculture was persuaded to change its statistical crop reports from "wine grapes" to "juice grapes." Many books written during the first quarter of this century referred in stinging phrases to the evils of alcohol, and made no distinction between wine and stronger beverages.

When the blow fell and the unthinkable actually did happen, there was great gloom in the wine country. As time went on, wineries folded, cooperages dried out and fell apart, and equipment was sold for junk. Growers began pulling out vineyards and planting their land to other crops, which they soon regretted. This was the era when prunes, apples, and walnuts became important crops in the Northern California wine country.

However, some strange, unexpected things were happening. Growers still in business began to reap a harvest by selling grapes to those who wanted to make "wine" at home. An obscure clause in the Volstead Act permitted the making at home of "non-intoxicating" grape juice for the homeowner's own use, to the extent of two hundred gallons a year. The price of grapes, instead of falling, went up. Thousands of tons of fresh grapes were sold, ostensibly to home winemakers, but actually to off-the-record bootleggers, chiefly in New York and other eastern cities. The demand was great; growers were delighted; business picked up. The price of grapes went from $10 a ton to $100.

Simi—Old farm equipment wheels on knoll above and behind winery.

Each winemaker tried to find a way to carry on.   J.H. Wheeler, a Napa County grower, began to convert juice into grape syrup, which sold mainly to soda fountains. Beringer Brothers Winery dried its grapes, installing evaporators and made a dry product which sold for 15¢ a pound.   Grape prices were soaring—the 1920 harvest, far from not finding a market, brought $80 to $100 a ton for red grapes.   Alicante Bouschet, a hardy red grape, brought the high price of $105 a ton.   Red grapes were the wanted varieties;   white grapes went for $50 a ton and less.

Like many others, Georges deLatour at Beaulieu replanted his splendid vineyard of fine wine grapes to varieties suited for shipment in 1922.   In spite of making money, however, growers and vintners alike believed and hoped that the good old days would return and bring an end to this madness;   some were surviving, but many were not.   The industry was on its knees.

In 1926 there was a short crop, and at the same time, prices fell.   Bootleggers had found that indeed liquor was quicker, and also more lucrative;   the price they got for a small amount of hard liquor exceeded what they could get for a much larger amount of wine.

Windsor Winery—Cooperage and dining area from balcony.

In the same year, the U.S. Attorney General ruled that home-made "wine" was legal "provided it was not intoxicating." This left a large loophole for home winemakers. Some wineries began selling a "wine brick" of condensed juice which came with printed instructions for making it into a beverage. These words were a part of it: "After it is made into a liquid by the addition of water, care must be taken not to leave it in a warm place, or else fermentation might occur and turn it into wine, which would be illegal." Some bricks were accompanied by a yeast tablet, with a warning not to use it as it might hasten fermentation.

The grape growers who were supplying these needs hurried to graft their fine wine grape vines that had survived over to the hardier varieties which would ship well for a distance of three thousand miles. Alicante Bouschet was the grape of the moment. Not only did it ship well, but it had the further quality of deep red skin and juice, and could be extended to make as much as six hundred gallons of "wine" from a ton of grapes (a normal average is about 130 gallons per ton).

When the fine wine grapes were replaced by mediocre varieties incapable of making good wine, the result was lower wine consumption by the wine-wise. People accustomed to drinking good wine had no good wine to drink. What was available through the corner bootlegger was of such inferior quality that the thoughtful wine drinker, accustomed to fine vintages, was virtually phased out.

The high prices lasted through 1925; by 1926 the flurry of wine grape shipping was over and California growers and vintners began exploring the possibilities that were left to them. One of these was the local making and sale of "grappa," a rough, crude red wine that was sold by bootleggers to the consumer whose only requirement was that it be something alcoholic. Another product was "Jackass Brandy." There were many stills made and put into operation in obscure corners of the counties; wine too poor to be sold as such, plus any other odds and ends around the winery, were distilled into a salable product whose only merit seems to have been that it was intoxicating, and a change from bathtub gin.

While the government as a whole did not see fit to take any responsibility for the fact that many had had their livelihood taken away, they did attempt some relief aimed toward warding off bankruptcy. In 1927, halfway through the Prohibition era, growers were being paid $5 an acre by the government to tear out their vines. Many accepted the offer. A government plan to salvage grape surplus by selling it as concentrate for home winemaking, already being done by many, ran head-on into pressure from the drys and had to be suppressed. The name of this product was "Vine-Glo," and it was being widely advertised when it was squelched by those determined that nothing tending toward salvation for grape growers should succeed.

In 1930, the Federal Farm Board and California banks lent nearly $25 million to convert surplus grapes into raisins and grape concentrate to be reconstituted into non-alcoholic juice. But the latter could not compete with the eastern grape juice; wine grapes with their delicately flavored juices were ignored by those who preferred Welch's. There was a short crop in 1931 which aided the growers, and by 1932 it was plain that an end to Prohibition was in sight.

During these eleven years, wine people struggled for existence by fair means or foul. The innovative tried to discover new uses for grapes, and several by-products were dreamed up, but income kept on decreasing. Bootleggers had found liquor much easier to handle and turn a profit on than supplies of Dago Red. To try to pull something out of the wreckage, growers' cooperatives were formed. One grower received $36 per ton for his crop through his cooperative; picking and transportation costs left him a profit of $88 for an entire carload of grapes.

By the 1930s the Great Depression was also making itself felt in California, where it was a comparative latecomer. Many vineyards were mortgaged as owners struggled to stay afloat. More grapes were pulled out and the land used for pasture, since many of the growers had been so badly hurt that they had no money to replant other crops.

Some fortunate wineries were permitted to make and sell sacramental wines. Georges deLatour, Beringer Brothers, both in Napa County, and Concannon Vineyards in Alameda County were among the fortunate few given this privilege. Their clientele was limited to the clergy of the Roman Catholic Church. Altar wines had always been Concannon's main product, and kept the winery going during Prohibition. Every five years for the rest of his life, reports wine writer Leon D. Adams, Captain Joseph Concannon expressed his appreciation by sending a gift barrel of his finest wine to the Pope in Rome.

Some wineries made money with medicinal wines and even tonics, especially when it became known that if they were thoroughly chilled, the noxious medicants would sink to the bottom, leaving a drinkable wine to be decanted from the top.

Road houses were popular places. There the adventurous young and the avid drinkers could go to wine, dine, dance, and make merry of an evening. One of these was at what is now Winery Lake, where the rye grown on the land was converted into rye whiskey and served to the customers who came out for a night of revelry in this obscure spot.

Another place, popular with the young, was Stag's Leap Tavern, now the site of a flourishing (and legal) winery. It was then a good place for what was known as "making whoopee," and even otherwise respectable members of society were said to sometimes take advantage of some, if not all, of its offerings, which included cabins for ladies of the night, located discreetly at the rear.

Old blower engines, at the old Louis Martini Winery.

There were numerous arrests. "We all did some bootlegging in those days," admits one old-timer grower and winemaker who survived the disaster and is now a respected member of the wine community. One local historian says that if all who were then engaged in illegal activities were arrested, there would not be enough jails to hold them.

Hundreds were fined; some served jail sentences while thousands of gallons of liquor and wine were confiscated, not all of which was virtuously poured down the drain by the law. In more than one county the sheriff was the bootlegger, thus neatly disposing of legal problems.

The liquor was often Jackass Brandy. The police were frequently involved, and the local bootlegger or tavern owner needed to make his own private arrangements with whatever branch of the law had jurisdiction. This could usually be done with considerable ease if a few of the right palms were crossed with a suitable amount of legal tender.

There was little respect of persons; records show that district attorneys' brothers and sheriffs' sons were arrested and fined, even jailed, if protection money was not forthcoming. Pockets of many law enforcement officers were lined by those operating outside the law, and the local operators of illegal enterprises were almost certain to have made sure the law was looking the other way. The speakeasy was a saloon or bar where only people the proprietor knew were admitted. This was more or less loosely complied with; in some quarters, it was sufficient to say "Joe sent me," or some other agreed upon password, to get in and enjoy the flow of spirits and wine.

Sometimes these dens of iniquity were raided and patrons and operators alike hauled off in the Black Maria, to be fined or incarcerated. Sometimes a raid would produce a bird in the net, worth real money to some law enforcement officer who might be persuaded to let him, or her, go and keep the name out of the newspaper. The speakeasies were mostly just a place for social drinking with cronies. Sometimes, though, they were operated in connection with rooms upstairs equipped with girls of easy virtue for the pleasure of one bent on a real spree.

A woman in Pope Valley, famed as the only lady bootlegger on the local scene, was raided one night by a sheriff's posse. She had her big still in operation, and plenty of product on hand. She freely admitted her guilt, saying it was her only way to make a living. She was arrested, fined $50, and told to mend her ways, or worse might befall her. She apparently went ahead with the next batch as soon as the posse was out of sight.

None of this is denied by anybody today, although some do not seem inclined to talk much about it, but smile an enigmatic smile. For a number of years after Repeal, the local wine growers and wineries preferred that their jousts with the law be ignored as they struggled back to respectability in their profession. Until the past couple of decades it was not considered polite or wise to refer to such things in the wine country. Now that time has dimmed the memory of those dark days, it has become de rigeur to boast that one's grandfather was a bootlegger, just as in earlier times people liked to brag about how grandpa was a pirate and made people walk the plank.

At Repeal, in June 1933, some 790 wineries were bonded overnight. Many of them were owned by former bootleggers to whom the government granted amnesty, provided they paid their taxes on current stocks. Much of the wine was spoiled and had turned to vinegar. All of it

Mayacamas—Front entrance, with dog.

was poor.   The industry remained in a depressed condition.

It must be remembered that this occurred at a time when the federal government felt no responsibility for the havoc its law had created for so many. If Prohibition had occurred forty years later, the situation would have been vastly different; the state would have been declared a disaster area, and Federal money would have been poured in by the millions to save the floundering economy and get growers established with other crops. But it was every man for himself. If some of the methods used to survive were frowned on by society, perhaps the perpetrators may be forgiven, for it is man's instinct to survive, and if the boat is sinking, any straw that floats by will be snatched up.

Although the pre-Prohibition era was a time when some excellent wines were being made by the descendants of Captain Gustav Niebaum at Inglenook, by Georges deLatour at Beaulieu, and a few others who held the line for quality, many California wines were shipped in tank cars, to be bottled in other states. They were often improperly handled, so that quality and reputation remained low. With this dismal picture so prevalent, and most wines within the states still being dispensed by "bottle houses," where one brought his own bottle to be filled, it is not surprising that the few really good wines went unnoticed by any but the most determined connoisseurs.

When the industry took stock of its position at Repeal it found itself with vineyards planted to poor varieties of wine grapes, with inadequate cooperage to use for fermenting, with few well-trained winemakers, and without a reliable and effectual distributing system. There were no wine waiters in hotels and restaurants. There were no wine merchants to advise and teach. Worst of all, there was no wine-conscious public familiar with good California wines. The battered industry was obliged to pick up the pieces and begin to build anew.

Did any good come out of Prohibition? Herbert Hoover called it "a noble experiment." Noble or not, if it was supposed to stem the tide of drinking in America, it certainly failed. And it had two effects which linger to this day. It resulted in much more, and younger, drinking by the young, who learned in high school to carry a pocket flask on a date. And it resulted in less respect for the law in all segments of society. The feeling that it is all right to break some laws is still with us today.

Chapter XI
Rebuilding the Wine Empire

Jacob Schram enjoys a glass of wine on his desk.

Following Repeal, the road back to prosperity for the wine industry was thorny and long. Everything was in such disarray that it took until about 1960 for the industry to get back on its feet, and even bigger and better than ever. At first, however, the winemakers were few, the grapes poor, equipment and cooperage lacking, and defeat and pessimism on the part of winemakers, rampant. Would it be any use to try to build again? Added to all this, the nation was in the throes of the Great Depression.

The wine industry in California is more than two hundred years old, but this figure does not take into account the many interruptions suffered during that time. Phylloxera lasted about twenty years; Prohibition and its effects another twenty. Recovery from both took time. There have been at least a dozen times when prices went down, grapes were pulled out, and winemakers hung on grimly or quietly folded and found other fields of endeavor. Perhaps the industry may be said to be around fifty or sixty years old, in actual time.

At Repeal seven hundred California wineries were bonded overnight, and laws went into effect that served to handicap the struggling industry still further. Some of these laws are still in effect today. Twenty-five states imposed import taxes on table wines at rates from 50¢ to $1.50 per gallon. Although New York, Ohio, and Missouri were also winegrowing states, these taxes were largely meant for California wines, since the state was the greatest shipper of wines.

When these taxes were added to the Federal tax of 17 percent, it succeeded in pricing table wine out of the market for many, and making it a rare luxury. Even today, some twenty states forbid the sale of table wines in grocery stores, which makes it inconvenient for the shopping housewife, the main purchaser of wine. Some states had within their boundaries dry areas; some counties have made it illegal to sell wine at all. In some states, restaurants are not permitted to sell wine with meals, which cuts their sale tremendously.

At Repeal there was little demand for table wines. People had become accustomed to drinking for the "kick," and table wine, made to be consumed with food, was not the beverage to supply this cheaply. Fortified dessert wine was, and it soon became the tipple of "winos" on the Skid Rows of the nation's cities. At that time, dessert wines were classified as "fortified" because they might legally be strengthened by the addition of brandy up to 20 percent alcohol. This made the fortified wine cheaper than hard liquor with its Federal tax, and thus the habitual drinker became dependent on dessert wine for his spirits.

At Repeal there was a whole generation of Americans who were completely unaware of the civilized pleasure of sipping a fine dry vintage wine with their food. They had become a nation of hard liquor drinkers, accustomed to buy whatever the bootlegger was offering, from moonshine whiskey to Jackass Brandy or Dago Red. The new generation of wine drinkers was totally unaware of good wine. To them it tasted sour, and of course many of the post-Repeal wines were sour and harsh, for little remained of the many great dry wine grape vineyards. They had been grafted over from delicate wine varieties to coarse, hardy, thick-skinned grapes which shipped well and brought a good price from eastern customers, but made poor wine.

In Northern California's wine country, populated largely by Italian Swiss, Rhineland German, and French ethnic background families, the people were always confirmed wine drinkers. They continued to drink their own home-made wine during Prohibition, and had little use for commercial wine.

The industry was in a slump, which is not to be wondered at; there was no good wine for those who wanted it. People were not accustomed to drinking wine with meals, and wine-indoctrinated families were well able to supply their own.

Another reason for the flagging demand for California wine was the many articles and books written by wine snobs, which gave some fearsome rules for serving wine. Americans hate to look foolish or stupid; rather than risk making social blunders they refrained from drinking wine or serving it in their homes. Sometimes the brave would timidly order a glass of wine in a restaurant, but this was likely to be in an Italian restaurant to accompany spaghetti or other hearty food, and the wine no better than it should be. Hence, nobody had an opportunity to become accustomed to wine drinking except those who had been drinking it from their cradles.

The industry itself took a dim view of its prospects. In a nation of whiskey drinkers, they felt their chances were slim.   The Federal Government, under the teetotaler President Herbert Hoover, was largely unaware of California's dilemma.   However, in 1935 there was an overlarge crop of wine grapes to be dealt with.   This inspired Dr. Rexford Tugwell, Assistant Secretary of Agriculture, to attempt to get better yeast strains from Europe.   Through his efforts to aid the industry, two model wineries with modern equipment were built in the Eastern U.S. to assist winemakers in re-equipping and restoring their crumbling facilities.   However, when this came to the ears of the redhot Prohibitionists, they squelched the project.   In spite of the fact that the more liberal Roosevelts had replaced the Quaker Hoovers, nothing further was ever done with the splendid building and its facilities.   The fine equipment was taken down and sold as government surplus.

Speaking of this period in history, Leon D. Adams notes in his book, *The Wines of America,* that during the first years after Repeal the very word "wine" was taboo. The Department's scientists feared to utter it, and "would look around furtively before even mentioning juice!"

The shortage of trained winemakers was another deterrent to recouping the losses of the industry.   Good winemakers of the past, whose wines had been acclaimed for their excellence, had found jobs of other kinds in other industries.   They felt that their new situations offered greater security prospects than winemaking with its unpredictable future.

As a matter of great good fortune, help was on the way.   The fifty-three year old University of California School of Agriculture was still intact.   This had been established in 1880, and its special mission was to teach and conduct wine research on its Berkeley campus.   Its first head had been Professor Eugene Hilgard, who had helped the industry through the phylloxera period.   He was later succeeded by Professor Frederic T. Bioletti.   The department had been struggling to come up with something that could be made from wine grapes other than wine.   The juice of wine grapes is not flavorful as is Concord grape juice.   The department was trying with fruit extracts, juices, and jellies to evolve salable products.

Bioletti quickly returned the emasculated winemaking courses to their original orientation, and was soon graduating enologists to take charge of winemaking in the newly opened or re-opened wineries.

During this period the University blossomed. The School of Viticulture and Enology moved its campus in 1935 to the Agricultural School at Davis, a practical farming school purchased by the University in 1906. It provided much more extensive acreage, and 140 acres of vineyard was planted and an experimental winery established. Since then the demand for graduates from this fine school has been great. A school of Viticulture and Enology was opened at Fresno State College in 1958, and it has graduated some enologists who are winning recognition in their profession. The noted winemaker Joe Heitz was on the faculty of this school for several years before founding his own winery.

In the decade from Repeal to 1945, great strides forward were made by scientists in this department. In 1933 Professor Bioletti hired a young geneticist, Harold Olmo, and gave him a free hand with an important project, with which he is still involved. It was the cross-breeding of grapevines to create new varieties and improve standard ones. His most important work has been with his crosses developed to produce fine wine grapes in less ideal climates than the North Coast counties of the state.

His has been a long, patient task. It takes about eighteen years to develop a new grape variety, from its first setting out to the time it has proved itself capable of realizing its full potential, and can be set out in a new vineyard. After that, it is up to the vineyard manager.

Over the years, Dr. Olmo has chosen, from tens of thousands of grapevines, the best producers of the finest varietal grapes, trying them in different soils and climates until, from among the many, he selects the few that meet his requirements, and new grape varieties are born. Two of the Olmo hybrids have enjoyed great success—Ruby Cabernet and Emerald Riesling, both of which are being grown in quantity in the fertile valleys of the San Joaquin. Another more recent newcomer is Flora, which is grown successfully in the warmer regions, and also in North Coast vineyards, where its grapes make a delightful light table wine.

More than one hundred thousand different grape varieties grow in the U.C. Davis vineyards. Among these are some one thousand from the principal named varietals that are cultivated in winegrowing regions of the world. The rest are the Olmo crosses and seedlings, undergoing testing for future work in the field.

Sterling—General view of the winery from just below the tasting-room sundeck.

The new grape varieties, hybridized and tested by Dr. Olmo, have much to offer to those planting new vineyards, for they are disease-resistant, and have evolved their special characteristics by cloning. This means selecting vines that produce grapes with definite mutated characteristics desired by grower or winemaker. Cuttings are taken from the chosen vine, and grown in the nursery until ready to set out in the vineyard. In this way, the best characteristics of each individual vine can be isolated and propagated. With these special clones, the grower can be sure of the qualities his grapes will have.

Plants are heat-treated in the University nursery to rid them of disease, and certified grapevines are available from the mother block at Davis or from several nurseries which specialize in disease-free grapevine stock.

The preparation of soil to free it from insect pests and destructive fungi has also been studied, and determinations made, by Davis scientists. All this information, plus help to put it to practical use, has been made available to the post-Repeal grower.

One of the most valuable things that came out of this research was the knowledge of fitting grape variety to climate. Added to this was the important finding that climates too hot make grapes loses acidity, while too cool results in low sugar, thus preventing proper balance in the wine. What makes good wine is good sugar-acid balance, and all vintners strive to attain this.

Dealing with California's always inadequate water supply has become more successful since the development of the drip irrigation technique. This conserves water by placing drip emitters between the bases of each two plants in the vineyard. Frost control by means of overhead sprinklers is another new development which has come out of post-World War II research. Wind machines to break up the inversion layer and bring warmer air down to the vines has replaced the burning of straw, old tires, and smudge pots that served the pre-environment-conscious grower. The knowledge of micro-climates within the vineyard; the practical uses of land contour and sun exposure, are all grower techniques that have come about in the same period. These methods of handling vineyard operations gradually came into general use as they were made available by the constant work of plant scientists, for effort was, and is, continuously made to improve methods and upgrade crop quality.

Although some of the new procedures have involved considerable expense, they are welcomed by growers as land and crops become more valuable and costly year by year—too valuable to leave anything that can be controlled by science to the hazards of chance. For it has been learned by scientists and men in the field alike that everything in the environment influences grapes, hence wine, and that none of these influences can be ignored or neglected by the grower of superlative wine grapes or the maker of great wine.

In 1935 Dr. Winkler, who succeeded Dr. Bioletti as head of the viticulture department, hired a graduate enologist, Maynard Amerine, who was just completing his doctorate. Amerine might well be called a one-man wine revolution, for he has had a tremendous impact on the industry, probably more than any other man save Haraszthy, and perhaps Andre Tchelistcheff, in wine history. He spent forty years working at U.C. Davis, traveling and lecturing, writing treatises and books on wine and winemaking. For this he has received many honors and won national acclaim.

Robert Mondavi—Exterior view from courtyard.

His first assignment in his new job was making experimental wine. Working with his boss, Dr. Winkler, he made a long series of tests, taking grapes from many areas of the state. Amerine says he often picked the grapes himself by day, keeping each picking separate, and made them into wine at night, carefully segregating each specimen. He studied, tested, and evaluated the results. Altogether the two made twenty thousand batches of wine during years in research. His first written report was in 1944—the first of more than three hundred works authored by the great scientist.

Tests convinced Amerine that the reason for California's continued wine mediocrity lay in the grape varieties themselves. So many fine vineyards had been ruined by grafting to poor varieties during Prohibition— that was the difficulty. Amerine set himself to turn the industry around and head it in the direction of quality; by dint of prodigious labors, infinite patience, plus nearly perpetual motion, he succeeded in doing it.

This required a tremendous program of education among growers; farm advisors had to convince them that the only way to go was to pull out the inferior grapes and plant to the finest, the truly great varietals. This was the only road to quality in wine.

Educating the public is slow work, especially when effort and expense are involved. Amerine and his assistants were on the road constantly in all winegrowing areas of the state, spreading the word, demonstrating techniques, encouraging, and explaining. Grape growers are farmers, and farmers are not known as innovators, quick to take up the new. But Amerine persevered.

In a few years things began to look up as the better vines began to bear, and the grapes made into wine. The evidence of the palate is incontrovertible—the better grapes did make better wine.

When the good varietals began to be harvested in quantity, it generated a trend among winemakers away from making generic wines, which had been the practice, toward making more varietal wines from their now fine grapes, worthy of bottling and aging. This was destined to change greatly the public image of California wine for all time.

Amerine's work included research on techniques and cultural practices: how grapes ripen, when to pick, color extraction, good yeast strains, the importance and technique of field sampling. Taking grapes from vines at exactly the right time is important, and the grower has the tools to tell when the time is right. This is possible by determining the sugar acid ratio to be found only by field sampling of a large number of vines.

The danger of overcropping to get a bigger yield was also stressed. Grapes will not ripen properly if overcropped, and the practice of "pruning long" to get more grapes always lessens quality. With quality down, wineries get poorer grapes, the price goes down, resulting in fewer and better grapes in ensuing crops, until the cycle repeats itself once more. There is one fact on which all scientists agree—the winemaker is at the mercy of the grapes.

After two years spent in the army during World War II, Amerine returned to the University, where he redoubled his efforts to raise the standards of the industry. He believed that its future would become more and more technologically oriented, and he and his staff traveled the state to provide growers with the scientific know-how they needed.

During this period (after 1945) growers finally began looking toward U.C. Davis as a place to go for guidance. The enological staff worked continuously with the

Dr. Maynard Amerine.

Hanzell Winery, near Sonoma. Exterior view of main winery building from entrance road.

wineries. The farm advisors in each area were industry-oriented, trained in viticulture and enology. The industry at this time needed the prestige given it by the University, and through this association, received much-needed impetus and became more sure of itself and where it was going.

Amerine also worked to bring about a more united voice for the wine industry. The Wine Advisory Board came into existence early in his career, making more research money available. Now there was both interest in wine and money to insure its future. Davis enrollment went up fast after the war, and vintners became better trained in proper winemaking methods. The University stays close to the industry to this day; there is a constant effort to meet the needs of growers and winemakers. Short training courses and workshops are offered for the busy vintner in need of instruction, with the added advantage of mingling with and talking to other members of his craft outside his area.

It became clear to Amerine, in evaluating grapes, that the climate in which grapes were grown was a very important factor. Dr. Amerine and Dr. Winkler embarked upon an ambitious classification of climates within the

Sebastiani—Gondola being dumped (this type rides on a flatbed truck instead of being the usual trailer-type).

state, dividing the California grapegrowing districts into five regions by their average climate during the growing season (April-October) and by comparing them to the wine districts of Europe. Understanding this helps to explain the wide differences found in the qualities and prices of California wines from various regions.

The light-yielding, delicate, costly grape varieties, which make the finest table wines, develop their finest flavors and character when grown in valleys near the coast, where warm, sunny days are cooled by ocean breezes and fogs. The hot climate of the state's fertile interior valleys yields magnificent clusters of luscious grapes, beautiful to look at, but making a bland characterless wine which must be given the needed lift by judicious blending.

The premium wine districts are, in order of coolness, known as Regions I, II, and III. To these, most of the land in Napa, Sonoma, Mendocino, and Monterey Counties Counties belong. The Northern San Joaquin Valley, further inland, and the Sacramento Valley, are classified as region IV. The warmest of all, the southern San Joaquin, is classed as Region V. These warmer climates are ideally suited to the growing of table and raisin grapes. But with the help of the University scientists, they are now able to grow wine grapes developed for their needs, and make them into good everyday wine.

Dr. Amerine was chairman of the Department of Viticulture and Enology from 1957 until his retirement in 1962, and he is still active. Retirement has not meant much to this vital, energetic man. He travels to all winegrowing regions of the state and the world. He is active in many wine-related organizations with which he is identified. He was recently honored by the American Society of Enologists. He has studied abroad under a Guggenheim Fellowship, learned languages (including Russian), and has received many awards from foreign governments for his contributions to the industry. During his career he has had the satisfaction of seeing the California wine industry come from the bottom both economically and in terms of quality, to challenging the fine premium wines of the world. He has seen winemaking become a prestigious and lucrative profession. Bradford Webb, well known wine consultant of California, notes: "In 1949, when I came to the area, a winemaker had no more prestige than a shoemaker." Dr.

Amerine has seen this change—winemakers, especially fine winemakers, are accorded the greatest respect, amounting almost to reverence.

Most wineries that had their beginnings in the period from the Repeal of Prohibition to the present have been encouraged and nurtured through their infancy by men such as Dr. Amerine and his colleagues. The industry owes them an enormous debt of gratitude.

Besides the academic influence, there is another that has had great impact on the industry—World War II. The war took all kinds of men from all kinds of backgrounds all over the world. Many of them lived, for varying lengths of time, in wine producing and wine drinking areas. While there, the ambience of wine crept into their awareness. They found it good to sit at the table with friends sipping good wine while enjoying food, conversation, and laughter. No one can drink a little wine without wanting to know more about this pleasant beverage; to be aware of it at all is to desire to know it better. Quite often, by the time men returned to civilian life, the habit of wine with meals was firmly a part of their life style, to be conveyed to family and friends.

The new affluence of the 1950s and 1960s influenced many Americans, young and old, to travel as they had never traveled before. Along with their elders, students in droves began crowding airports every summer, fired with desire to see and experience other ways of life besides their own. Formerly, travel had been for the wealthy. Now it was available to the farmer, the plumber, the storekeeper, the housekeeper, the housewife, and above all, to the student. The coming of jet air travel during this period has also played its part in the increased popularity of wine.

The travel boom further brought home to Americans what the drinking of a pleasant wine can add to the enjoyment of food, especially when shared with family or friends. Many Americans have finally escaped from their parochialism into the maturity they have sought, as a people, for a long time. They have found out that the world is filled with many pleasant things, and that it is a high time they experienced as many of them as possible.

All these influences coming along in sequence brought on the 1960s wine explosion, which has served to put the state's premium wine regions on the map and make California wine country as well known as Europe's.

Chapter XII
The Wine Explosion

Beginning in the middle 1960s, the wine explosion made itself felt in California almost overnight. From one day to the next, it seemed, there were new wineries under construction on every hand. Northern California had twenty five wineries in 1950; two decades later there were more than one hundred. New wine books, and books on every conceivable wine related subject, popped up on bookstore shelves. Every daily paper sprouted a wine column for the benefit of its readers. There were courses in the appreciation of wine offered at universities. There were innumerable wine and food clubs. Wineshops staffed by more or less knowledgeable wine merchants sprang up. Suddenly, everywhere wine and the wine country became the "in" thing, and winemakers the beautiful people.

Actually it was not as sudden as it seemed. Wine consciousness had been coming on quietly and subtly for years—ever since the end of the war. For it was about this time that good California wine became increasingly available. This upgrading of quality went on quietly for some time before it was generally acknowledged. Gradually more people became exposed to wine; one member of a group began to enjoy drinking wine and indoctrinated a few friends.

Ideas changed slowly, and many old ideas persisted that had to be overcome before a wine boom could be launched. It had been considered the thing to downgrade California wine, and it was done religiously by the envious and the timid, those afraid of seeming provincial. Wine had for years been seen as a beverage for low castes. To admit that one drank, even enjoyed, California wine was to admit an eccentricity, or worse.

This attitude was at one end of the scale. At the other end was the snobbery from which evolved wine protocol rules as inflexible as the Ten Commandments. Those who served wine in the wrong glass, or served the wrong kind of wine with the roast were looked down upon with scorn. Envy of the upper crust, and fear of committing a faux pas in their presence, kept many potential wine drinkers from making any attempt to drink wine.

The new enjoyment of wine crept on nevertheless, almost person by person. The idea that cultured people drank Scotch while the low brow and the peasant drank sour red wine was slowly waning. Meanwhile the wines became better and better. A more scientific approach to grape growing and winemaking came to be the norm in California wine country, and the days of the untrained winemaker were over.

The industry itself had for some time felt the need for promotional effort. In 1935 The Wine Institute began putting a small levy on its members to accumulate funds for promotion. The Wine Advisory Board was established under the State Department of Agriculture to administer this fund, which was sizeable—about $4 million per year. Part of this money went for research, as in the past, and the rest went into promotion.

In the first years of the wine explosion, most people involved with the industry were not wealthy. Some wineries opening at the beginning of this era had struggled years for existence. The fact that they were making really fine wine went far to get them out of the red, coupled with the new, if subtle, industry promotion. As Dr. Albert Winkler, professor of Agricultural Economics at Davis, remarked in 1967, "The new wine drinker with an informed taste for good wine did not just suddenly appear, like Venus on the half-shell. He is the result of quiet but persistent industry promotion."

Dr. Andre Tchelistcheff, master winemaker and consultant, in his favorite place—the barrel aging room.

There was none of the Madison Avenue touch about wine promotion. Promotional efforts, appropriate for launching a new car or new cigarette, were frowned upon by the finest winemakers. They wanted their product to speak for itself. Promotion was so low key that it was not seen as promotion at all. But due to influence, the list of wine enthusiasts began to grow, and continued to grow. It became possible to offer a glass of wine as an alternative to hard liquor at parties. A group of young people picnicking on a grassy bank, passing a jug of wine from hand to hand provoked smiles from onlookers, instead of startled and contemptuous stares.

Before 1966, when the wine explosion actually got under way, there had been few wineries established in Northern California since Repeal of Prohibition in 1933. Fred McCrea and Lee Stewart, both involved with big business, founded small, excellent cellars, Stewart in 1943, McCrea in 1953. These men were of a new breed in wine circles. They did not come from wine backgrounds, but were merely people who wanted to change to a more agreeable way of life. They came to winemaking because they wanted to do something that would give them personal satisfaction, provide a challenge, money, and an opportunity to live away from large centers of population. They knew they would need help, and looked for it in the right places. They went to University of California scientists, farm advisors, and men already in the field. They began by getting the best equipment and selecting the finest grapes from carefully selected stock. They knew their new life would not be easy but they were prepared to make a total effort as the price of making great wine.

Actually it was wine quality that turned the trick and induced the wine boom. The whole thing would have been impossible without great wine being made for the new wine enthusiast to drink. Most of the wineries began to bottle and age their wines in the 1940s, instead of selling them in bulk as had been the custom for years. U.C. Davis labored long and hard to give the industry the tools it needed. Winemakers trained at Davis or a new prestigious school of enology. They knew how to achieve good color, stability, clarity, nuances of flavor, aroma, and balance in their wines. These were dry table wines, not the ports, sherries, and dessert wines that had been the mainstay of the industry during and since Prohibition.

If one incident can be singled out to mark the beginning of the new era it was the construction in 1966 of the Robert Mondavi Winery in Napa County. Robert Mondavi was determined to found his own winery apart from the family business, and he built a large facility, of Mission architecture, designed by a famous architect. He equipped his winery with the finest winemaking machinery that could be gleaned from this country and Europe.

At about the same time, in Sonoma County near Santa Rosa, former dancer Rod Strong decided it was time to hang up his dancing shoes and concentrate on expanding his small wine business he had established in the basement of his home in Tiburon, near San Francisco. At Windsor, north of Santa Rosa, he built an immense structure in the shape of a huge X, and began his expansion program.

Strong's promotional idea was the original one of personally labeling his wines. Customers found this a means of enhancing their own self image, and flattered friends liked to receive a case of wine with each bottle marked on the label, "Bottled expressly for the pleasure of John Henry Doe." His winery flourished.

Far Niente Winery after restoration in 1983. Napa Valley.

Then wineries began to spring up like mushrooms after a rain. They went from a meager thirty-three wineries in Napa, Sonoma, and Mendocino Counties in 1968 to over one hundred in the same area by 1978. The wine industry began to look very good indeed to people who had always wanted to operate their own business. The new wine men were often those who had already become interested in wine, some of them for years. Others had been hobby winemakers.

Many of those who founded the small, prestigious wineries that constituted the new crop had been involved with some segment of big business, and had found it economically rewarding but inimical to quality of life. Long hours spent in the corner office, no matter how many Oriental rugs were underfoot, did not offer scope for the person or food for the spirit. It was stiflingly uncreative; they longed for a change to create something of value uniquely their own.

The stories of the founding of these wineries show a certain similarity as, one by one, men like Jack Davies at Schramsberg, David Stare at Dry Creek Vineyards and Donn Chappellet at Chappellet Vineyards left their accustomed and highly lucrative paths to embark on new ventures in the world of wine.

Davies labored long and hard to bring his champagne into the prominence it bears, and deserves. He was thoroughly disenchanted with his life as a Southern California corporation man, and has found a much more rewarding life for himself and his family as a result of his change to a champagne maker.

Stare, a Harvard graduate from Boston, with an academic family background, left an enviable life situation to begin a winemaking adventure in California. He built a winery which has produced some notable vintages, acclaimed here and abroad, after studying enology at U.C. Davis.

Donn Chappellet was a Southern California businessman who started a small business and three years later found himself with three thousand employees. He fled the scene, and traveling about Napa Valley by plane, located a spot near Lake Hennessey where he planted hillside vineyards. He built a winery shaped like a pyramid, one side merging into a hill, where he has made some excellent vintages. It has taken him years to achieve his present status.

Winemaking is a business—part science, part art—that does not evolve and blossom in a day. Years must be spent in learning, gaining experience, upgrading, tasting, evolving, trying, rejecting, and spending money before a winemaker finally arrives. These men would not say they had arrived, for greater excellence is always ahead, and the most successful of them still strives to better a fine performance.

These are the attitudes that make the North Coast the home of fine dry table wine. As wineries proliferated, land was cleared of other crops and readied for grapes. Prices went up; good vineyard land became scarce and very valuable, and grape prices went to fantastic heights.

The decision was reached by those who grew grapes that only the best should be grown on these precious acres. They were too few acres, and it was too costly to grow the old types of grapes.

With all the assistance available from research and education, with all the dedication that growers and winemakers can muster, and with the economic situation as it is today, is is a small wonder that the grape growing areas of California are planted to the finest of premium dry wine grapes. These plantings are pedigreed vines, watched over by dedicated vineyard managers, many of them Davis or Fresno graduates. The vines are cultivated by the most approved scientific methods for securing top quality crops, and wineries vie with each other in securing them for the production of superior wine. Vineyards become as famous as wineries for the excellence of their products, and names of famous vineyards often appear on fine wine labels.

The new wineries that have come into being since the wine explosion are devoting themselves to the making of fewer wine varieties of special characteristics, instead of a full line of table, dessert, and sparkling wines, as was the custom just after Repeal. Some wineries, such as Diamond Creek Vineyards in Napa Valley, are producing a single varietal wine, in this case Cabernet Sauvignon. The winery, however, bottles three different Cabernets grown in different areas of its small twenty-five acre vineyard, for soil analysis has revealed that each small section is different, and each capable of making a wine with fascinating differences from the others.

Some larger premium wineries produce three, four, or five prime varietal wines, feeling that this is all they can achieve while doing them the justice they deserve, for winemakers in the area have immense respect for their grapes. They understand that the potential for the wine lies in the grapes, for good wine cannot, by any skill of the winemaker, be made from inferior grapes.

The wine boom reached its crescendo in 1968 when the consumption of table wines outstripped dessert wines for the first time in California wine history. It now outsells them three to one. It was after that the planting rush began in earnest. Other crops—prunes, pears, walnuts, and apples—were pulled out to make room for grapes. Plantings to the prime varieties went ahead apace, and by the early 1970s, plantings of wine grapes covered most of the available agricultural land in California's North Coast, reaching its height in 1973.

Out-of-state investors had become aware of the North Coast wine industry. United Vintners bought several of the large family owned wineries whose reputations for fine wine had gone unchallenged for generations.

Other firms began offering fantastic sums for operating wineries, envisioning table wine as a great growth industry in its early stages. Nestle of Switzerland purchased Beringer Brothers, family owned for five generations. Widmer's of Naples bought a vineyard and built a winery in Sonoma County. Schlitz Brewing Company purchased a small winery, Geyser Peak, and began a large program of expansion. This small winery near Geyserville on Highway 101 is recalled for its small, puckish sign on the highway, reading, "No wine for sale. We drink it all."

Every old winery in the area, some long neglected and filled with debris and cobwebs, became a coveted property. Old cellars, converted to storage or other uses, were reopened.

Although old timers in the industry warned the over enthusiastic to tread carefully, remembering other "boom and bust" situations in the past, the state's winegrowing areas were over-planted in the late 1960s and early 1970s. But the experts at the University of California say this was a temporary condition in Sonoma and Napa Counties, where all the agricultural land could profitably be planted to wine grapes.

The price of grapes rose to unprecedented heights in the years 1971-1973. Top varieties such as Chardonnay and Cabernet Sauvignon were bringing the grower a price

Far Niente (restored). The fermentation area in the winery's second level.

in four figures per ton, with "points" added for extra sugar content.   The grower who watched his grapes carefully, had the cooperation of the weather, and harvested at the right time, could expect a top price for his best grapes.

In 1974, with more and more young vines coming into production each year, the disaster the doom-sayers had been predicting took place.   There was an over-supply of grapes, due to three bumper crops in a row.   The price of grapes zoomed downward, to bottom out at about $250 a ton for premium varieties.   Growers without winery contracts for their crops were in deep trouble, and wineries could be very selective, with grapes from prestigious vineyards waiting on their doorsteps.

The crunch came about because of the huge tonnage of grapes, and the inadequate facilities of the North Coast wine country to handle and process them.

The following year the price began to inch upwards, improving a little in 1975.   In 1976 and 1977, nature stepped into the picture and brought a drought to the wine country.   These two years of drought resulted in lower tonnage but increased quality;   the less water grapes contain, the richer the juice of the grape crop. Prices went up again, and growers began to feel more confidence in the future.   It must be said that the growers in the premium winegrowing areas, with few exceptions rode out the storm, never losing their firm belief in the unique quality of their grapes, and believing that quality alone, if held to religiously, would see them through.   It is their stout contention that there cannot be too many good wine grapes, or good wine.

The North Coast Grape Growers Association, formed of growers in the three county area some thirty years ago, vowed never again to let themselves be caught in a price bind.   They needed to own their own winery and storage facilities.   As they were looking for a site, Souverain of Alexander Valley Winery came on the market in 1976. The purchase was made, and the grower members see this winery, with two-and-one-half million gallon storage capacity and an efficient and well-equipped winemaking facility, as the answer to their problems, offering them a permanent and stable home for their grapes.   It is interesting to note that at no time was the lower price of grapes reflected in wine prices, which rose consistently during this period.

Growers and vintners of the area have now survived another major crisis of the industry, and feel that their position, at least for the foreseeable future, is strong. But there is yet another hazard, a direct result of the wine explosion.

Urban sprawl, always nibbling at the fringes of the state's agricultural lands, began more than two decades ago to gobble up land in the North Coast wine country. Some of the finest vineyard land in this favored by-nature spot, called by Luther Burbank "the garden spot of the world" was covered very quickly with concrete and rooftops.

To save the coast counties vineyards and preserve a green belt, a state law known as the Williamson Act, put into effect in the 1960s, provides for the creation of agricultural preserves, in which land is taxed on its value as farm land. This law came too late to save many vineyards, particularly in Santa Clara and southern Sonoma counties. Growers there were forced to move operations to new, climatically favorable areas in more sparsely settled regions, which brought the industry north into Mendocino County, and south into Monterey County.

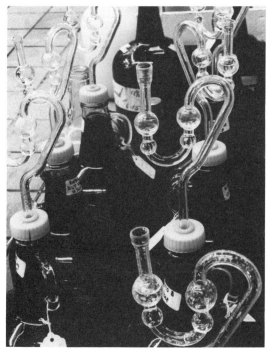

Robert Mondavi—Bottles of fermenting juice (experimental setup).

In 1968 the Napa County Board of Supervisors acted to set a minimum twenty acre agricultural preserve zoning law. This prevents plots of vineyard land from being broken up as subdivisions. This has been challenged in the court by land development interests, but at present the twenty acre minimum still stands within the preserve. The vintners now represent huge money interests, and have convinced the state Highway Department that they should consider alternatives to a projected new six lane freeway through Napa Valley vineyards, and they have abandoned the proposal at least for the present. This leads growers to believe that you can fight City Hall successfully, provided you have public opinion, expressed in loud, outraged cries, on your side.

Meanwhile, efforts go on continually to bring the newest and best that science and industry can provide to the aid of this burgeoning industry. U.C. Davis and Fresno State University have added new training programs and conferences on growing and making wine for the busy man, or woman, for the distaff side is now being represented in the industry. Research continues, and today the University serves as the chief American source

Robert Mondavi explains the fine points of wine tasting to guests.

of technical information in the fields of viticulture and enology. The research staff, augmented by well-trained scientists, has given renewed effort in field and laboratory. Perhaps the only area of winemaking where automation has not penetrated is in the vintner's palate; there is no substitute for this, and each vintner constantly studies, tastes, and evaluates wine as he strives to keep this needed tool keen.

Viticultural research on acid formation, effect of molds, maturity evaluation, development of hybrid varieties, influence of rootstocks, soil additives, irrigation, pruning, and other practices were augmented and accelerated during the wine explosion, and still go on.

The new importance of wine has lent an aura to the place where it grows. The area already has a special ambience, and everyone who visits there feels it. Wine people are thought to be the most gracious hosts in the world. And to the area as a whole, many things to augment the good life have been added.

In Napa Valley, at Inglenook, the winery owners (Heublin Inc.) have put together a museum of old pictures and artifacts, displayed in the old winery building. At Christian Brothers, the world famous corkscrew collection of Brother Timothy is exhibited. The entire collection numbers many hundred items, so only a portion of it is on view at one time.

In Beringer Winery, and also at Inglenook, Christian Brothers, and many of the old wineries are old screw presses, winemaking equipment, and vineyard implements, and many hand carved casks and ovals of great beauty and charm.

Due also to the influence of wine, fine dining has come to the wine country, and some delightful places to lodge. These two were in desperately short supply before the wine boom. Now really fine food, prepared by master chefs and served in surroundings of elegance and beauty, is becoming more and more available.

Wine tastings and wine and food events have great cachet and are the "in" way to entertain. Good restaurants and hotels now have wine lists which include some really fine California bottlings, rubbing elbows with the great wines of France and the world. There are good selections of California wines in liquor stores, and almost best of all, there are knowledgeable wine merchants to advise the beginning wine drinker. The Napa Valley Wine Library is a unique collection of wine related books, and is housed in a new, enlarged building in St. Helena. There are books for the wine buff, magazines devoted to wine and its adjuncts, and newsletters by wine men in the know, the latter available by subscription.

Those who know the pleasures of wine are naturally led to an appreciation of other fine things as well. Good books, fine paintings, and great music are on the wine appreciator's list of things to enjoy. Those involved with the world of art say that wine is a friend to the arts. It gives a capacity for eloquent, even noble thoughts, ably expressed. It has contributed to the creativity of poets and painters. It enhances the appreciation of art. In fact, those in the know say wine enhances and augments everyday experiences by heightening appreciation. It gives a subtle dimension to life, not a new one, but a deepening of a dimension already there. Drinking wine, it is said, is a civilized and civilizing pleasure.

All these things have been added to life as grapes and wine have come more into the consciousness and palates of more and more people.

Chapter XIII
The Circle Goes Round

Michael Topolos, winemaker, writer, and teacher, with his Russian River Vineyards winery at Forestville. It recaptures the rugged redwood buildings left by the Russians at Fort Ross.

Victor Hugo once said, "There is nothing so powerful as an idea whose time has come." In the mid-sixties, the time had come for California wine. This was helped by the greater affluence of the times, and by low-key, subtle promotion by the Wine Institute, which was founded thirty years earlier for this purpose. But the chief influence was the men who had vision, courage, dedication, and a dream of greatness for their wine.

Among those responsible for the momentum the industry received at that time were some inspired and determined men and women who worked to create quality wines that would not only make them successful, but add lustre to the image of California wine.

Among those responsible for the greatness of California wine are men who were not from winemaking families, but men who saw, in the wine country and the making of wine as a career, something that spoke to them. Many of them were formerly involved with the hectic pace of big business; the ambience of wine and the wine country lured them with the idea of how good life could be in its pleasant valleys and foothills, surrounded by the lush green vineyards.

There is something of the romantic in those who love the vine and its fruit, beauty and order, and have a desire for the continuity and balance of springtime and harvest, and the opportunity each year to create from the grapes something fine, perhaps even great. Winemaking is elemental, a part of mankind for many centuries. To become a part of this stream of history has enhanced the desire to become a maker of good wine.

The industry must acknowledge a debt of gratitude to some outstanding men for their achievements, their contribution to wine itself, and to the industry as a whole. Those men include, but are not limited to, Andre Tchelistcheff, Robert Mondavi, Leland Stewart, Fred McCrea, Joe Heitz, Jack Davies, and, a bit later, Donn Chappellet, Mike Grgich, Tom Burgess (who took over Stewart's original cellars), Charles Carpy at Freemark Abbey, Dick Arrowood at Chateau St. Jean, and many others. Each of them has honored his dreams of greatness for the area's wines in a practical way.

They believed, and still do believe, that California wine can look to a future of greatness that has virtually no limits, and they desire to be a part of the picture. They find no labor too arduous, no expenses too great for them to undertake in their quest for perfection. Theirs is a zeal to make noble wines and to see them become known and recognized by the great palates of our time.

Andre Tchelistcheff, the son of a lawyer, was educated

in enology in France, and came to Napa Valley to work for Beaulieu Vineyards in 1938. He is a scientist who believes in winemaking as a science as well as an art. Russian born and French educated, he has the Gallic love for the fine and beautiful, and this makes him an inspired teacher. He indoctrinates those he tutors with his own boundless enthusiasm for this craft. To him winemaking begins with the grapes, and as vintage time nears, he can walk through a vineyard without a refractometer and determine whether it is ready for harvest. During the thirty-five vintages he made in his years at Beaulieu, he had a tremendous impact on the industry. He brought with him from France the latest enological knowledge and viticultural research. He shared this knowledge and expertise with everybody in the area who wished to learn by founding an enological laboratory in St. Helena and training many young winemakers who later became producers of fine wines. After he retired from Beaulieu in 1973 he served as consultant to many wineries; the Tchelistcheff influence will be felt in California for many years and many generations to come.

He is a charter member of the American Society of Enologists, which began some thirty years ago for the purpose of creating professional standards for the industry, and to show the calibre of California winemakers in both viticulture and viniculture. Great thinking, dedication, and creativity, teamed with study and research—these have made the wine industry in California great. These ideals, he believes, will keep the state's wines great as long as the winemakers keep reaching for greater achievements.

One of his earliest students was Robert Mondavi, whose father, Cesare Mondavi, was a shipper of grapes in Lodi. Later Cesare made bulk wine at the Acampo Winery there. He began to assess the future, and came to believe that it lay in fine bottled wines, and that the finest of these would be produced in the state's North Coast valleys. His sons, Robert and Peter, elected to follow in their father's footsteps as winemakers, and to prepare themselves to make the greater wines they both added courses in enology to their college curriculum. Robert, who already held a degree in science from Stanford University, went on to study enology at the University of California School of Enology. He has achieved great personal success in his own winery, which he founded in

1966, the first of the new wineries which have proliferated since then.

Early in his career, he says, he was given two bottles of wine by Jack Daniels, then winemaker at the great Inglenook. These wines were made by Captain Gustav Niebaum. Because Bob was so impressed by the quality, he began immediately to lay the foundation for making similar wines himself. He worked for his father at the newly acquired Sunny St. Helena Winery, and later at the family winery, where they made wine under the Charles Krug label.

Bob Mondavi has made some outstanding vintages. But his chief contribution to the industry is his tremendous zeal for, and belief in, himself and the wine industry; not only his own, but all the fine wine being made in the state. He became a self-appointed ambassador of California wine. He traveled to New York, Washington, and other Eastern population centers, taking his wine to tastings where he presented it with great enthusiasm, which did much to put California wine on the tables of the wealthy and influential in the United States. He encouraged and advised many young men just coming into the wine industry, and many fine winemakers today are proud to say they got their start working for Robert Mondavi.

Never in all the years since he began has his zeal or enthusiasm flagged. His winery is also a center for the arts, and he sponsors concerts and the presentation of visual arts all year long. Today it is not too much to say that he may claim the title "Dean of Napa Valley Winemakers."

One of the men aided and encouraged over the years by Robert Mondavi was Leland Stewart. He came to Napa Valley in 1943, just retired from the hectic life of professional advertising. He wanted to lead the life of a country squire, but unfortunately he ran out of money in a few years. This canny Scotsman decided that by learning to make good wine, and by producing outstanding wine, he could make a living in the grand style he admired and intended to reach. He began with the small stone winery already on the place. Not having the advantage of a wine background, he went ahead without it. He found it was quite possible to make fine wine, given time, helpful friends, study, and grinding toil With the aid of Andre Tchelistcheff and the encouragement and advise of Robert

Chappellet using wine-thief (note bung and bung-starter).

Storybrook Mountain winery's carved oak cask, given by friends to owner Walter Schug when he opened the winery in 1984.

Mondavi, plus the help of the Department of Enology at Davis, he became a winemaker. He believed that technology is the great thing in making good wine, and two years later, in 1947, he made his first Souverain Cellars wine. He was an idea man; because it had never been done was no reason not to try, and on this basis he created and marketed the first varietal Green Hungarian wine. It won immediate acclaim, and has been a consistent winner at fairs and expositions. By making, tasting, and evaluating over the years he developed a fine palate, an indispensable asset to the maker of fine wines.

Lee Stewart began making wine as a means to an end—living the good life. He remained to value his accomplishment for itself. Stewart later sold his winery and it carries on under another name, but his career made an impact on the valley, and his influence lingers today. The name of Lee Stewart and the original Souverain Cellars is respected by the entire industry.

Another of the same breed was Fred McCrea, who bought Stony Hills for a summer home for his family in 1943. After a few years the McCreas began to clear and plant a small vineyard. The property is beautiful and secluded, and the stony soil and hilly terrain have proved ideal for grapegrowing. Fred McCrea was also an advertising man, and continued this career for years while he became a great winemaker.

It was a few years before the McCreas made their first wine in the family kitchen, and it was not until 1951 that they released their first commercial vintage. Meanwhile they got to know their winemaker neighbors, and winemaking slowly seeped into their blood. Fred considered the situation, talking with Robert Mondavi, Lee Stewart, and experts at U.C. Davis. The planting of the vineyard was an arduous task, all done by hand, for the steep terrain would not permit machinery. McCrea wanted to grown Chardonnay, but was warned by his University friends that it was a shy bearer and unpredictable as well. However, he elected to plant Chardonnay, and also Pinot Blanc and Johannisberg Riesling. The tiny winery he built was bonded in 1951, and Stony Hill wine has been on the most wanted list ever since.

Fred taught himself with the help of friends, and developed his own philosophy of wine tailored to the rugged terrain and the small winery. He read, he studied, he made wine. Wines from so small a winery are bound to be different, year to year, and he used this to his advantage. The Stony Hills reputation grew. During those first years Fred was his own winemaker. He proceeded to make such excellent wine that it was all snapped up each year by a waiting list of friends and wine buffs. Fred McCrea knew wine, as did his wife Eleanor, from rootstock to bottle on the table, and they enjoyed it thoroughly. They had found the ideal way to live, as well as the satisfaction of creating something beautiful and fine. Many a young winemaker has admired the Stony Hill winery as being exactly what he would like to have himself. Visitors are impressed by the tangled wildwood setting, the view, the small perfect winery, and the magnificent wines.

Fred McCrea was a big man, in stature, in concepts, and in ideas. He died in 1977, and left the operation of the winery to his wife Eleanor and to the young winemaker they had hired in 1962, Michael Chelini. The wines continue to be subtle, delicate, complex, as Fred himself created them. They are described by connoisseurs as having a subtle flavor rather than an aggressive intensity, a delicate balance, and a finish of understated elegance. The Fred McCrea influence lingers on in Napa Valley, where he was a much loved and respected member of the wine community.

Joe Heitz was stationed in Northern California in World War II, and he became acquainted with the state and its custom of wine drinking and wine appreciation. He was determined to become a part of the wine picture, after his military obligation. He moved to California in 1944, where he spent some years attending U.C. Davis majoring in Enology. For ten years he worked at Beaulieu, under the tutelage of Andre Tchelistcheff. Later, he set up the Enology and Viticulture Department at Fresno State University, and taught there for five years, making the school a mecca for enology students that has since become nearly as prestigious as Davis.

He decided he was ready for his own winery, and was able to buy the Leon Brendel "Only One" cellars at St. Helena, with eight acres of vineyard planted to Grignolino grapes, which was the "only one" wine made there. The small amount of pinkish orangey Grignolino Rose he made there could not support his family, and he capitalized on his rare ability to select lots from other

Chappellet Vineyards—Exterior, winery building.

wineries that he could improve by blending and aging. The quality of these Heitz selections, wines he made from his own vineyard and from carefully selected purchased grapes, attracted connoisseurs. He was launched.

The Heitz palate is famous. Experts and wine writers say it's the kind that happens only once in a lifetime. With this asset, and the help of his wife Alice, who studied and learned along with him, he has achieved a great reputation. Soon he needed more room; he was able to buy an old winery and house at the end of Taplin Lane near Rutherford. He equipped the winery with new machinery, presses and tanks, and racks of French oak for aging. He planted the vineyard to Grignolino, Chardonnay, and Pinot Noir. He continued to buy grapes from some of the most prestigious vineyards in the area, whose growers were glad to sell them to Joe Heitz, for under his skilled hands they would become the best possible wine. Many of his famous wines bear the name of the vineyard on the label.

Joe Heitz has become another of the men who held the line for quality and made it pay. He has built an additional winery building and the old house has been reconditioned into a home of great warmth and charm. Joe has also had the satisfaction of seeing his children want to follow the family tradition. David, a Fresno graduate, is now working in his father's business, and his daughter works in the family administration office.

Another of the men who has opted for making a small quantity of excellent wine is Jack Davies at Schramsberg Champagne Cellars, one of California's renowned cellars. The story of his adventure with wine is told elsewhere; the important thing about Davies is his devotion to excellence and his resolute turning away from anything that does not tend in that direction. He has never compromised with quality; such an idea is never a part of his thinking. "I want to make a small quantity of superlative champagne," he has said, and he has done exactly that. All of his vintages are superb, and all are made by the time honored Methode Chapanoise, slow and laborious. They are highly esteemed by wine lovers world wide.

Names on this roster could go on and on. Donn Chappellet, a former Los Angeles businessman, took six years to get ready to make wine. His grapes are picked into baskets, handled carefully, and made into very good wine by his enologist, Cathy Corison. Chappellet Vineyards makes only a few wines, but they are excellent. His pyramid shaped winery is unique, a cathedral of wine.

Mike Grgich, a winemaker from Yugoslavia, has been making good wine around Napa Valley for some twenty years, working for Bob Mondavi and other good winemakers before he founded his own, Grgich Hills Cellars. He has received many awards and medals for his wines, and is making his influence felt in the wine community. Each vintage is unique and interesting, and very, very good. He says, "This is a house of Chardonnay," and this is his most valued wine. His older vintages of this wine bring fabulous prices, and become better every year.

Tom Burgess, owner of Burgess Cellars, formerly Souverain, is a former commercial airplane pilot from the East. He has blended well into the wine scene, and his wines are winning acclaim from wine connoisseurs. He is named as a fine winemaker by no less an authority than Eleanor McCrea at Stony Hill, and has been the subject of magazine articles by reason of his outstanding vintages.

Charles Carpy is the son of an old winemaking family who heads a group of growers, owners of Freemark Abbey. The Freemark Abbey wines are nationally known, especially those from such prestigious vineyards as Bosche and Martha's Vineyard. The Cabernets are especially fine, and become fantastic with age.

Richard Arrowood, winemaker at Chateau St. Jean in Sonoma County, has also been making great wines for years. His white wines, particularly his Chardonnay, are different each year, with difference due to vineyard location, which make these wines of special interest to connoisseurs.

So many fine wines are being made today in Northern California that, as winewriter winemaker author-teacher Michael Topolos says, it is hard to find a poor wine for purposes of illustration in his classrooms.

Even the lesser wines produced in California today are, almost to a bottle, clean, fresh, and drinkable. Few are not up to this standard, at least not yet. The industry, as has been pointed out, is young. There is time ahead for improvement, and those who belong to the group of winemakers determined to keep bettering a fine performance are numerous, dedicated, and resolute.

Big money coming to the wine country in the middle

Unloading grapes by the crate at Chappellet Winery Grapes entering crusher-stemmer.

and late sixties has also made a needed contribution. These large corporations had money to spend for promotion. Trained, intelligent promotion men and national advertising have done their part to enhance the image of California wine world–wide. Aided by big money, the wine industry has acquired clout in legislative halls. This makes it seem likely that the wine valleys will remain vineyards, and not be give over to tract housing and industrial development.

More wineries keep opening all the time, and for the most part, their standards are high. It has become so costly to own and operate a winery in California today that none but the most affluent can afford to do so, and they are people with the money and the desire to create better and better wine.

There has been no attempt made to bring this story up to the present moment, for history is happening all around us. This is a chronicle for the wine–lover, to tell him just how it all came about. As it is hard to know where to begin a history, it is also difficult to know where to conclude it. The circle goes around, again and again, each year presenting the maker of wine with new challenges and new difficulties, creating new traumas and triumphs. The maker of good wine seldom if ever leaves the color and drama of winemaking for any other occupation.

And what of the future? Winemakers believe firmly in the future of wine in California, just as those before them did. Louis P. Martini, who grew up in winemaking, notes that the industry members themselves are optimistic about the future. "Right now," he says, "there is more California wine than can be marketed advantageously, but this is in the short term. It's a slow process, but new wine drinkers are coming into the picture every day, and in the long term, there will be more and more consumers of good wine. A winemaker has to take the long view."

Winemakers seldom retire; they die venerable and full of years and wine knowledge, handing the winery over to their posterity only when death slackens their hold on the reins.

Family wineries such as Martini, Foppiano, Sutter Home, could have sold out many times over, and their owners retired to a life of wealth and leisure. That they do not succumb to the lure of big money says that to these men there is something infinitely more precious and valuable—the making of good and noble vintages.

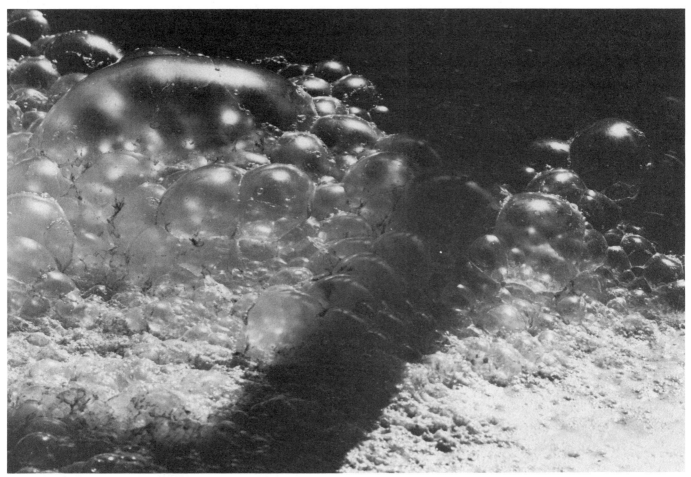

Beaulieu—Juice direct from the crusher.

ABOUT THE AUTHOR

Betty Dopson loves people, especially winemakers. A long career as a journalist has given her the opportunity to attend the birthing of many wineries. Her writing is serious, often witty, and lyrical enough to be called poetry.

Her first book, *Napa Valley Wineries*, was a great commercial success and set the standard for publications of this genre.

BIBLIOGRAPHY

Adams, Leon. *The Commonsense Book of Wine.* New York: D. McKay Co., 1956.
Vines of America. Boston: Houghton Mifflin Co., 1975-1977-1981.

Amerine, Maynard. *Wines, Introduction for Americans.* Berkeley: University of California Press, 1965.
Wines, Their Sensory Evaluation. San Francisco: Freeman Press, 1977.

Balzer, Robert. *Adventure in Wine.* Los Angeles: Ward Ritchie Press, 1969.
This Uncommon Heritage. Los Angeles: Ward Ritchie Press, 1970.

Benson, Robert. *Great Winemakers of California.* Santa Barbara: Capra Press, 1977.

Bentley, Iris. *Wine with a Merry Heart.* New York: Comet Press, 1959.

Boulleray, Yvonne. *California Wine Cooking.* Santa Rosa: Self-published, 1975.

Broadbent, J.M. *Wine Tasting.* New York: Simon & Schuster, 1970.

Carosso, Vincent P. *The California Wine Industry.* Berkeley: University of California Press, 1830-1895, 1951.

Colburn, Frona Eunice Wait. *In Old Vintage Days.* San Francisco: J. H. Nash, 1937.
Wines and Vines of California. Berkeley: Howell North, 1973 (reprint).

Critchfield, Burk H. *California Wine Industry During Depression.* Berkeley: University of California Press, 1972.

DeKovic, Gene *This Blessed Land.* St. Helena: Illuminations Press, 1981.

Dutton, Joan Perry. *They Left Their Mark.* St. Helena: Illuminations Press, 1983.

Eby, Gordon. *Napa Valley.* Napa: Eby Press, 1972.

Escritt, L.B. *The Wine Cellar.* London: Wine and Spirits Publications, 1972.

Fisher, M.F.K. *The Story of Wine in California.* Berkeley: University of California Press, 1962.
Cordial Water. London: Faber and Faber, 1963.

Fluchere, Henri. *A Golden Guide to Wines.* New York: Golden Press, 1973.

Gorman, Robert. *California Premium Wine.* Berkeley: Ten Speed Press, 1975.

Gould, Francis Z.L. *My Life With Wine.* St. Helena: Self-published, 1972.

Haynes, Irene. *Ghost Wineries of Napa Valley.* San Francisco: Sally Taylor & Friends, 1980.

Heintz, William. F. *Freemark Abbey Winery.* Napa: Self-published, 1975.

Haraszthy, Agoston. *Father of California Wine.* New York: Harper & Row. Reprint from 1862.

Jones, Idwal. *Vines in the Sun.* New York: William Morrow, 1943.
The Vineyard. New York: Duell Sloan & Pearce, 1942

Lester, Mary. *Hand Me That Corkscrew, Bacchus.* San Francisco: Piper Press, 1973.

Lucia, Dr. Salvatore. *Wine and Your Wellbeing.* New York: Popular Library, 1971.

Marcus, Irving. *Lines about Wine.* Berkeley: Wine Publications, 1971.

Martini, Louis P. *Louis M. Martini, A Family Winery.* St. Helena: Self-published, 1984.

Morgan, Jefferson. *Adventures in the Wine Country.* San Francisco: Chronicle Books, 1971.

Mowat, Jean (editor). *Anthology of Wine.* England: W. H. Houlder Shaw.

Norman, Winston. *More Fun with Wine.* Wine Advisory Board, 1972.

Palzer, Lyman. *History of Napa and Lake Counties.* New York: Slocum Bowen & Co., 1981 (Reprint).

Pellegrini, Angelo. *The Unprejudiced Palate.* New York: McMilliam & Co., 1948.
Wine and the Good Life. New York: Knopf, 1965.

Ramos, Adam and Joseph. *Mixed Wine Drinks.* 1974
Robert Mondavi of Napa Valley, 1979

Parker, Tom. *Inglenook Vineyards.* Napa: Privately printed, 1979.

Roberge, Earl. *Napa Wine Country.* San Francisco: Graphic Arts Center, 1975.

Rossi, Edmund B., *Italian Swiss Colony and the Wine Industry.* 1971.

Schoonmaker, Frank. *Dictionary of Wines.* New York: Hastings House, 1951.

Sbarboro, Andrea. *Fight for True Temperance.* Privately printed, 1914.

Stevenson, Robert Louis. *Silverado Journal.* New York: Dutton and Co., 1954 (Reprint)

Topolos, Michael and Dopson, Betty. *California Wineries,* Napa Valley. Napa: Vintage Image, 1974.

Wagner, Philip M. *Grapes into Wine.* New York: Knopf, 1976.

Waugh, Harry. *Bacchus on the Wing.* London: Wine & Spirits Pub., 1966.
Diary of a Winetaster. New York: Quadrangle Books, 1972.
Pick of the Bunch. London: Wine & Spirits Pub., 1970.

Wechsberg, Joseph. *The Best Things in Life.* Boston: Little, Brown & Co., 1968

Wente, Ernest B. *Winemaking in Livermore Valley.* Berkeley: University of California Press, 1971.

INDEX

PHOTO CREDITS

All photographs are courtesy of the following:

Beaulieu Vineyards: 59, 109

Jay Bjerkan: 30, 98

Alfred Blaker:
27, 32, 39, 66, 68, 70, 71, 73, 74, 77, 87, 88, 91, 92, 95,
96, 101, 103, 105, 106, 115, 121, 123, 125, 127

California Historical Society, San Francisco: 7, 65

Charles P. De Crevel: 118, 122

Far Niente Winery: 49, 110, 113

Inglenook Vineyards: 42-45

Loaned by Gaye LeBaron: 69

Robert Mondavi: 40-41, 116

Sonoma County Museum: 2, 4

Wine Institute:
3, 7, 8, 10, 11, 13, 14, 18, 20, 23, 24, 26, 29, 33, 36, 42,
46, 52, 55, 61, 62, 63, 67, 72, 78, 80, 83, 84, 104

Special thanks to Alfred A. Blaker for sharing many photos from
his personal collection.